CONFRONTING THE CONTROVERSIES

A Christian Looks at the Tough Issues

Adam Hamilton

ABINGDON PRESS
Nashville

This book is printed on recycled, acid-free paper.

Library of Congress Cataloging-in-Publication Data

Hamilton, Adam, 1964-
    Confronting the controversies : a Christian looks at the
    tough issues / Adam Hamilton.
        p. cm.
    ISBN 0-687-04567-3 (alk. paper)
        1. Christian ethics—Methodist authors. 2. United Method-
ist Church (U.S.)—Sermons. 3. Sermons, American—20th
century. 4. Christian ethics—Sermons. I. Title.

BJ1251 .H26 2001
241.0476—dc21   2001022389

04 05 06 07 08 09 10—10 9 8

MANUFACTURED IN THE UNITED STATES OF AMERICA

CONTENTS

FOREWORD

Adam Hamilton is my pastor. He is a remarkable pastor and preacher and one of the most gifted leaders in The United Methodist Church today.

Two years after completing seminary, Adam was appointed to start a new congregation. Today, The United Methodist Church of the Resurrection (COR) is one of the fastest growing mainline congregations in the United States. This church (and Adam himself) is as complex as many of the issues he writes about in this book. You seldom find just what you expect. While many megachurches downplay their denominational identity, this church makes denominational identity obvious and important. Those who come from churches where they have experienced traditional worship find COR to be innovative. Those who visit from churches practicing contemporary worship find COR fairly traditional. People who see themselves as conservative find Adam a bit liberal. Those who call themselves liberal see a clear evangelical direction.

But all experience in Adam respect for people and their beliefs. This pastoral concern permeates *Confronting the Controversies*. Biblical and theological foundations are vitally important, but the pastoral task remains utmost in Adam's mind. These are not, finally, ideologically driven pronouncements. They are parallel to the way John Wesley preached from a pastoral perspective. He worked as hard as anyone ever did to know what true doctrine was. Yet when Wesley stood to preach, he did not begin with the true doctrine. He began with the particular congregation to which he was speaking.

After hearing a tape of the sermons out of which this book grew, someone who does not agree with Adam on some of these issues said, "These messages are nothing short of remark-

5

able—especially in the way Adam lays out positions other than his own." Adam works very hard at seeing a debate from the perspectives of those who hold the differing beliefs. This is indeed a gift. It is tempting for us to present *our* position in the best light, while representing opposing positions in stereotypical or unflattering terms.

When we abandon the tension between opposing viewpoints, we are no longer leading toward a greater truth. We are merely partisan advocates for a part of the truth. This is one reason the church and our society have not been served well by either the Old Left or New Right. Each takes partial truth with no tension and presents it as the whole truth.

Among the great strengths of this volume is Adam's ability to hold positions in tension and to bridge the gaps that exist between people. Well-meaning Christians have sometimes been the source of *greater* division and distrust. While desiring to include some, we have, through some of our practices, made others feel unwelcome around the table.

You will find in these messages humility alongside conviction. Adam acknowledges that his own views on these issues may very well change in decades to come. History teaches us all humility. No single branch of the Christian family, no one theology, no particular political stance, has had a monopoly on justice and freedom. If anything, history shows how much we need to learn from one another. Righteous pride can make it harder to see the shortcomings of one's own positions. We need each other, for God's wisdom is never found totally in any one place among God's people.

How many more might experience the community of faith if we could hold together conviction and humility, passion and perspective. May this book become a model for us—that our own convictions may become stronger and deeper, even as we grow each day in our respect for others for whom God has not revealed wisdom in the same way.

Lovett H. Weems Jr.

INTRODUCTION

Do you have an opinion on the death penalty? What about physician-assisted suicide? Do you feel strongly one way or another about abortion? Or homosexuality? Chances are you do have strong feelings about some of these subjects. Regarding others you may have opinions, but you haven't spent a great deal of time thinking through the issues.

For many of us, if we are honest, we would admit that our opinions are often shaped either by our parents, by our friends, or by compelling stories we have heard. Sometimes we hold certain opinions because people we respect hold those opinions. Or we may hold a position because someone we do not like holds the opposite position. Sometimes we see a film or read a book that persuades us in one direction or another, though often we find it difficult to articulate all the reasons why we hold a position. Then too we sometimes find it impossible to understand how anyone could hold the opposite opinion. Many of us don't really take the time to think through what we believe until we have a personal experience—sometimes a crisis—that forces us to weigh the consequences of a difficult decision. Polls show that many of us don't even choose our leaders based on their positions on the issues; we are more likely persuaded to vote for candidates by their personalities.

On important social or moral issues we find people sharply divided. These issues create walls and barriers that divide families, friends, and even churches. Often we do not know how to dialogue on important issues. If we're not careful, we demonize those who hold views in sharp contrast to our own.

How did you arrive at your positions on those issues you feel strongly about? How do you feel when confronted with someone who holds the opposite opinion? In what ways has your faith informed your position?

Our faith, as we will see, can have an important role in shaping the values and morals that we pass on to our society. Our opinions matter, and our thinking on the hard questions of our time will have an impact on the shape of our future. If we have considered the complexities of these issues in a community of faith, prayerfully seeking the guidance of the Bible, our tradition, and the leaders and experts who can inform us, we are more likely to be ready both to meet a personal challenge that requires us to make a difficult decision and to offer a meaningful contribution to the deliberation of our nation.

In response to the current state of divisiveness and bitterness I felt led to preach a series of sermons at The United Methodist Church of the Resurrection in Leawood, Kansas, entitled, "Christianity and the Controversial Issues of Our Time." My goals in preaching this series of sermons were:

1. to help Christians learn how to do Christian ethics; that is, how to think through complex moral issues applying both biblical teaching and theological thinking to these concerns;
2. to provide a model for how to dialogue about moral issues and maintain respect for persons on both sides of the divide;
3. to teach both Christians and non-Christians how the Christian faith relates to critical issues in contemporary society; and
4. finally, I had the same goals for this series of sermons that I have for every sermon that I preach, namely, to evangelize, encourage discipleship, offer prophetic challenges, and provide pastoral care to my flock.

There are, to be sure, more in-depth books written on each of these topics. The limitations of what can be accomplished in the context of a thirty-minute sermon are evident in the pages of this book. At the same time, there is evidence that these sermons had a significant impact on the life of our church and the lives of the people within our congregation. We had numerous stories of unchurched persons who came to worship simply out of curiosity or by the lure of hearing someone speak about something controversial, but who in the end found themselves drawn to Christ as we offered them a picture of the power of the Christian life, while dispelling many of their preconceived ideas about Christians and the Christian faith. In many cases those who were committed Christians reported changing long-held views on the issues presented or at least gaining an appreciation for those who held views that were opposite of their own. Finally, worship attendance increased dramatically, indicating a great interest on the part of both members and visitors.

How These Sermons Were Written

My own interest in the field of ethics was developed in seminary at Southern Methodist University's Perkins School of Theology. I am indebted to Dr. Joseph Allen who brought logic and clarity of thought to the field. My love for ethics was rewarded with the senior award in social ethics upon graduation. More than this, I was left with an intense desire to pursue doctoral work in the field. My work in the pastorate will likely keep me from seeking another academic degree, but it does provide me with the opportunity to continue to study, reflect, and teach ethics in the "real world" where people actually make life-and-death decisions.

Never have I preached a series of sermons that required more preparation in the form of study, reading, reflection, prayer, and then writing and rewriting multiple drafts of each message than did this series. I spent an average of twenty hours preparing each sermon. I had the benefit of an insightful staff team with whom I would dialogue on Monday morning about the topic to be tackled that week. In addition, my assistant, Sue Thompson, did a marvelous job of filling my files with research from the Internet, which added immensely to the body of information I had the opportunity to incorporate into each message.

Some have wondered about the wisdom of preaching on controversial issues in the local church. "Won't this divide the church?" "Aren't you afraid of people leaving the church?" "Are you ready for the angry letters you will receive?" These are all questions people asked as we prepared for this series.

These are not the kind of sermons pastors should preach in their first few years of ministry in a church. There are some churches where a pastor could never preach a series like this. But part of the joy and benefit of serving a church for a long period of time is the opportunity to do things that may be a bit risky. I was in my tenth year of ministry at the Church of the Resurrection when this series was preached. The people in our congregation had come to know my love for them, and they trusted that I would handle these sermons with respect and care.

The truth is, the response to these sermons was overwhelmingly positive. We made an announcement about the upcoming series at our Christmas Eve candlelight services when we have a large number of unchurched people in attendance. We felt that this was a series of sermons that nonreligious and nominally religious people would be highly interested in returning for. We printed a full-color postcard listing the title and date for each sermon in the series. At the end of each candlelight service we drew attention to the postcard and gave a brief promo for the series, which started two weeks later. We also mailed the postcard to everyone on our mailing list.

The result was that worship attendance increased from forty-two hundred in worship per weekend in November, to over fifty-two hundred per weekend in January, an increase of more than one thousand per weekend! We built up to the most controversial issues of abortion and homosexuality. On the last of these sermons—on homosexuality—we had more than six thousand people in attendance.

More gratifying than the numbers was the heartfelt response of the people. They thoroughly enjoyed this series! People throughout the community were talking about these sermons. Our members and visitors talked about them at work, with their neighbors, and among their family members. They invited friends to come to worship like never before. Most of our members said that even when they disagreed with a conclusion I might offer, they still appreciated the sermon and it helped them to grow.

That is not to say that we did not have some negative fallout. Of the forty-five hundred members we had at the time, we may have lost as many as five or ten over the issue of these sermons. I received more than four hundred e-mails in response to the sermons, but only thirty or forty were negative. Before preaching a series like this the pastor must be prepared for criticism. But for every critical e-mail or letter, I received many more that were appreciative and encouraging. Over all, our members indicated genuine respect and appreciation for their pastor and his willingness to tackle these issues.

A New Approach to Controversial Issues

A large part of the success of this sermon series in accomplishing the goals laid out above, and the reason why it prompted enthusiastic support, was the basic approach taken to the controversial issues. I hope that this approach will become apparent in each sermon as you read it. The approach begins with certain basic presuppositions often lacking in the discussion of these issues in society, and in the church.

My first assumption is that what makes an issue truly controversial is that it is a complex issue, not prone to simple and easy solutions. Because it is complex and multifaceted, a controversial issue by definition will result in multiple perspectives. An even more important assumption is that thinking,

11

compassionate, and caring people of faith can hold opposite positions on these issues. That does not mean that both are right, but both may have appropriate motives for holding their opposite perspectives and both will likely have valid points to make in the debate. Finally, some of these issues will be impossible to resolve completely this side of eternity.

This entire set of assumptions and my approach to these sermons can be summarized in two words: sensitivity and respect. In order to address adequately the topics in this series I had to understand not only the underlying issue but also the arguments on both sides of the debate. I am grateful for my training in forensics and debate in high school. In one form of competitive forensics opponents are required to take various social issues and to argue persuasively for or against a particular position. We were not always allowed to choose which side we would take on the issue we were arguing; instead, we were charged with presenting the side we were assigned—even if we disagreed with it—with such integrity, reason, and passion, as to persuade the judges of the validity of this position. This exercise prepared me in many ways to preach this series of sermons; and perhaps more important, it prepared me for understanding people.

Another key element of my background and training that helped me appreciate both sides in a debate was my own spiritual journey and my theological schooling. I came to faith in Christ in a conservative church and in this church heard a call into ministry. My undergraduate degree in theology and pastoral care was from a conservative university. My seminary training, however, was firmly grounded in the more liberal traditions of the United Methodist school of theology I attended. What I came to see in each of my degrees was that there are elements of truth on both sides of the great theological and sociological divide, but those on either side had a hard time hearing or respecting those on the other. This experience helped me appreciate and look for the truth in both sides of difficult issues. I have tried to practice the discipline of placing myself in the shoes of those who hold strong opinions on both sides of a debate.

This leads to a key component of addressing controversial issues from the pulpit (and in many other arenas as well): People of opposite perspectives want to feel that their position was heard, respected, and accurately represented. Parishioners become hurt or frustrated when a pastor speaks to a complex issue and argues persuasively for one side while failing to adequately represent the opposing view. This is especially the case if one has not taken fully into account the deep motivations that guide people's opinions and convictions.

I was told again and again during this series that even when parishioners disagreed with me they appreciated the way I presented their viewpoints. The reader will notice that in most of these sermons I used the same formula: I begin by presenting, as objectively and persuasively as possible, one position. About ten minutes into the sermon I then move to the second position. Again, I present this position with respect and passion. Finally, I devote the last ten minutes of the sermon to summarize and present my own views as a fellow Christian seeking to wrestle with the issue.

I would encourage the reader to consider purchasing the audiotapes of these sermons in order to capture the intensity and emotion of these messages. There are also elements that are included in the sermons as they were preached that were not possible to capture in writing. This book was designed to serve both as a resource for preaching and as a study guide for adults who wish to think through theses issues in groups or as individuals. Those who use this book as a reference for their own preaching should, of course, take the formula as a guide but carefully craft the sermon with the needs of their own congregations in mind.

If the book is used by a Sunday school class or an adult study group, the videotaped copies of these sermons—each about thirty minutes in length—will be most helpful when the class uses them as an introduction to be followed by thirty minutes of discussion. Congregations are likely to have members who work in fields related to these issues—medical personnel, public-school teachers, employees of the criminal justice system, for example—who can serve as additional resources for the study group. Some preachers may find it helpful to use this book with a group of interested and informed members for discussions *before* a series of sermons is written and preached as well as with follow-up groups who want to continue the conversations. We had wonderful discussions in Sunday school following each sermon at our own church as I preached this series.

The purpose of this book is to help us consider controversial issues in the light of the Bible and Christian beliefs. The point is not to give you *the* definitive Christian perspective on any of these issues. Controversial issues are by nature complex and divisive. Good people get upset about them. On every topic we cover there will be well-meaning and thoughtful Christians on both sides of the issue. My aim is to help us, as Christians, to consider the issues in the light of biblical teaching. For too long only the churches on the extremes of the theological spectrum have discussed some of these subjects, offering radically liberal or radically conservative perspectives. Seldom do churches in the center attempt to wrestle with these issues. My hope is that this discussion is an opportunity for you to grow in your faith, learn more about the Bible, and develop your own informed perspectives.

I want to express my appreciation to Abingdon Press for their encouragement and enthusiasm in bringing this series of sermons to print. My hope and prayer is that this book is helpful to you, the reader, as you seek to grow in your faith and allow Christ to form and shape your views. I make no claims that the views represented in the conclusion of each sermon are the definitive word of truth from God. I suspect that some of my own views will change on these issues in the decades to come. They do reflect the best efforts of one pastor trying to relate the timeless truth of the Christian faith to the ethical and moral challenges of our time.

Gracious God, we thank you for the courage of those who came to our land seeking freedom to worship you; may we treasure that freedom and grant it always to others. We thank you for the love of Creator and creation that we learn from those who lived here first; may we prize the gift of their reverence for all that is truly yours and seek forgiveness for all that was taken from them. We thank you for the hope of those who were brought here against their will, surviving fearful wrongs and planting themselves in the garden of your grace; may we remember their suffering and praise the power and beauty of their presence. We thank you for the persistence of those who come still today from east, west, north, and south: the tired and the poor, the oppressed and the neglected; may we welcome them as your Son welcomes all who come, embracing them no longer as strangers but as friends. In Jesus' name; Amen.

CHAPTER ONE

The Separation of Church and State

"You are the salt of the earth; but if salt has lost its taste, how can its saltiness be restored? It is no longer good for anything, but is thrown out and trampled under foot.

"You are the light of the world. A city built on a hill cannot be hid. No one after lighting a lamp puts it under the bushel basket, but on the lampstand, and it gives light to all in the house. In the same way, let your light shine before others, so that they may see your good works and give glory to your Father in heaven." (Matthew 5:13–16)

Remind them to be subject to rulers and authorities, to be obedient, to be ready for every good work, to speak evil of no one, to avoid quarreling, to be gentle, and to show every courtesy to everyone. (Titus 3:1–2)

❄   ❄   ❄   ❄   ❄

How Do Christians Decide What Is Right and Wrong?

How do you begin to develop your positions on important moral issues? Most people do not spend hours reading over the various ethical debates. We do not usually do our own research. Typically, our personal experience, the convictions of others we trust who study the issues, the beliefs of our parents and others who have influenced our lives, and what we read in magazines or hear and see on television, radio, and in the movies help shape our views. Many of us simply don't have strong opinions on various issues. We often know what we *don't* believe, however, and those negative reactions are based in part on how little we like the purveyors of those views.

But for us who call ourselves Christians, our views, positions, and beliefs should all spring from our understanding of the will of God. Christians seek, above all, to know and do *the will of God.* Ultimately, nothing matters more than this. God has created us, has a plan for us, and we believe we will be held accountable for how we respond to God's will. We consider ourselves citizens of God's kingdom first, even before our national citizenship, and we strive to live so as to bring God's reign to the whole world. When we invite Jesus to be Lord in our lives, we invite him to be our sovereign or ruler. We agree to live by his commands and teachings. And we pledge to seek to do his will.

As we struggle to understand God's will in our lives, we know that God does in fact care about all of the issues we will address in this book and the people who face them. Can anyone who is a believer truly think that God does not care what we think regarding criminal justice and the death penalty? Or euthanasia? Or how homosexuality is looked at and how homosexuals are treated?

Some people have suggested that these are merely "secular" issues. But though *we* make distinctions between what is sacred and what is secular, *God* does not. The Bible says, "The earth is the LORD'S and all that is in it, the world, and those who live in it" (Psalm 24:1). For God, all issues, all circumstances, and all people are a part of God's domain. Separating the sacred from the secular is a false dichotomy.

Wesley's "Quadrilateral":
Four Tools for Discerning God's Will

So then, if God does care about these issues, and if we as Christians long to know the heart of God, where will we go to discover God's will? How can we discern the convictions God would have us hold and work toward? John Wesley, the eighteenth-century founder of Methodism, offered four tools for discerning God's will. In our time we call this the Wesleyan "Quadrilateral" (quadrilateral means "four sided"). These four principles will be the tools we'll use in this book as we consider the issues before us:

1. *Scripture:* The Bible is the primary means for learning God's will; we study the Scriptures prayerfully, looking for precepts, principles, and direct commandments as they relate to the issues at hand. The Bible is our map, our guide, our "owner's manual." But the Bible can be difficult to interpret. It was written in a time when circumstances were very different from ours; and sometimes, confusing us further, the writers express perspectives that seem to conflict with each other. But, remarkably, most often the Bible speaks to us with one voice about what God expects of our lives. To help the Bible speak to us more clearly, we also turn to the Christian tradition.

2. *Tradition:* Along with the Scriptures, we look for guidance to the teachings and beliefs of the church as expressed by Christians in all ages. The Christian tradition includes writings about theology and doctrine, prayers and liturgies, the writings of councils, and the wisdom gained throughout Christian history. Tradition, for those who are United Methodists like myself, also includes the *Book of Discipline* and the *Book of Resolutions* of The United Methodist Church, as well as John Wesley's writings. As

United Methodists we may not always agree with our denomination's official positions, but they must, at the very least, be taken seriously in forming and shaping our understanding of God's will. God speaks through thoughtful church leaders through the ages.

3. *Experience:* The experience Wesley refers to is not simply a collection of events and happenings, which may not always present a reliable picture to go by, but our experience of the Holy Spirit working in our lives. We experience the Holy Spirit in worship, in the fellowship of other believers, and in our work and testimony for God's kingdom in the world. In other words, we believe that God speaks to us through the Holy Spirit's witness, discerned through prayer and confirmed by our experience with the community of disciples.

4. *Reason:* Wesley believed that God gave us the ability to apply reason to our interpretation of God's will. Reason by itself can be manipulated and lead us in the wrong direction—it is obviously possible to make a "reasonable" argument on either side of an issue—but reason can be used along with the other three tools and be constrained by them.

These are the basic principles and tools that we will use in these discussions, and I would encourage you to use them every day as you seek to discover God's will for your life, to see all aspects of your life through the eyes of faith. They can help us view all issues through the eyes of faith. Our task is to be informed, to understand the issues, and to seek God's direction for us. Regardless of how you come out on a given issue, my hope is that you will seek God's will and long to bring your convictions in line with your faith, so that in all things Jesus Christ may be Lord in your life. And through our study of these topics, I hope that we all grow in our faith and that together we can work toward a more just society.

19

What Is the Role of Individual Christians and the Church in Influencing Culture?

When we speak about moral issues and the separation of church and state, we must talk about culture because culture offers an even more significant reflection of our values than does the government. The main conflict in our country isn't over liberal or conservative governments or Republican or Democratic leadership. Political parties and elected officials are merely a reflection of the culture that shapes them.

What is culture? *Merriam Webster's Collegiate Dictionary* defines culture as "the customary beliefs, social forms, and material traits of a racial, religious, or social group." Culture includes the dominant worldview of the people living within it: How do they look at the world? How do they make decisions? What are their foundational beliefs and values? How do the people spend their time, and how do they entertain themselves? From the "culture"—the common values, beliefs, ideals, and worldview—come the arts, humanities, laws, and the "state."

Culture is like wet cement; it will be shaped by *something*. Individual Christians and communities of faith can and should play a role in shaping the culture. Though we live in a society in which a vast majority of people claim to be Christians, our culture has become increasingly influenced by non-Christian values and ideals. Too often, on important issues, the vast majority of churches and Christians are silent, allowing those on the more vocal and often more radical edges of the theological and sociological spectrum to define the debate and the culture for us. More often we have capitulated to the news media and to Hollywood, allowing them to become the dominant forces in shaping our culture.

The hopeful news is that our culture can, of course, be influenced and shaped by the beliefs and practice of genuine, thoughtful, and committed Christians. We believe that the values of our culture matter to God, and because they matter to God, we are expected to seek to understand God's will and pursue it. As Christians, our role is to think through these issues, to live our lives according to our beliefs even when they run counter to the culture around us, to bear witness to the truth as we understand it in the marketplace of ideas, and to make a plausible case for our values and ideals.

Since culture is shaped by our beliefs, which, in turn, are shaped by what we put into our minds and hearts, it is crucial for Christians first to commit ourselves to growing in the faith. Christians are meant to be shaped by the spiritual disciplines, including Scripture reading and prayer, worship and the sacraments, study and Christian fellowship.

It's not easy to resist the influences that are so pervasive in our culture and that are competing with the church for our attention. Children left to choose without guidance often watch television programs that depict conflicting values. They may be caught up in the struggles of TV's teenagers or attractive young adults who do not operate from a Christian worldview. They may watch shows that are saturated with gratuitous violence and focus on careless sexual activity, and their cultural values and morals are formed in this atmosphere. The culture wars are being fought over what we are willing to allow our children to see, to read, and to listen to.

H. Richard Niebuhr was one of the great Christian ethicists of the last century. In a book that remains a classic introduction for many students of Christian ethics, *Christ and Culture* (New York: HarperCollins, 1986), Niebuhr seeks to look at the biblical relationship between Christians and the culture. He summarizes five different models: Christ *against* culture, Christ *of* culture, Christ *above* culture, Christ and culture *in paradox*, and finally, Christ *the transformer* of culture.

Each model has some biblical support to commend it to us, but it is the last, Christ the transformer of culture, that seems most exciting and most compelling to me. The concept that Christ, working through his people, can be the transformer of culture strikes at the heart of Jesus' words in Matthew 5:13-16 where Jesus tells us that we, his followers, are to be salt and light. Salt transforms the physical properties of that which it

21

touches. It brings out the goodness in food and was used as a preservative that kept meats from spoiling. It is essential for life and it has certain healing properties. Jesus had all of this and more in mind that when he challenged his followers to be salt. Imagine the impact that the church—and we as individual Christians—might have on our culture if we were truly being the salt of the earth! What would this look like? And what of light? We are called to be light for the world—a city set upon a hill that cannot be hidden. A flashlight illuminates the right path through the woods on a dark night, showing the potential pitfalls along the way. A lighthouse offers guidance and warning to keep the ships from certain peril. A night-light brings comfort to my daughter as she goes to sleep each night. Daylight allows us to see the world as it really is. There seems to be no shortage of dark places in our world—where the blind seem to lead the blind, or where people live in fear, or are in constant danger of shipwreck. How important that there should be beacons of light, showing compassion, care, and a purposeful and illuminated life for others to see.

The church and individual Christians, at their best, have often played a tremendous role in shaping the culture, and in turn in shaping the state. The church, at its best, has championed the causes that recognize the value and worth of human beings. It has pursued freedom in the face of slavery, the right of all persons to earn a living wage, and the provision of equal access to education and the vote, along with concern for children, the low-income family, and the physically and spiritually ill. Although the United States is not officially a "Christian nation" and has always rejected the formation of an official state religion, it has been heavily influenced by Christianity and Christian virtues and worldviews. Those characteristics that we are most proud of in our nation's past were, in large part, the result of people of faith seeking to be salt and light—seeking to shape and transform their culture and world.

The church's influence is never accomplished easily. Nor is there ever complete success. But each situation involves Christians struggling to distinguish right from wrong and seeking to nudge the culture closer to the foundation of our worldview. For this task we find our source of strength in the Holy Spirit, in our beliefs, and in the support of the community of faith. But to adequately engage in this calling to be transforming agents in our culture we must have absolute clarity about the relationship between the church and the state.

The Relationship Between the Church and the State: The Constitution

Let us first consider the constitutional issues that are the primary source of much consternation on the part of some Christians.

The first mention of God or religion in the Constitution is found in Article Six, where we read the following: "No religious test shall ever be required as a qualification to any office or public trust under the United States." This prohibition does not prevent voters from choosing candidates on the basis of religion, but it does mean that a particular religious perspective cannot be a state mandated prerequisite for any public office. An atheist, a Christian, a Buddhist, and a Satanist can all legally hold office in this country; no one can be disqualified by the state because of his or her religious affiliation or lack thereof.

Individual voters are, however, allowed to ask questions about and to know a candidate's religious persuasion, and this information can and should be a factor in determining whom we vote into public office. Why? Because one's religion shapes everything else about that individual; it shapes worldview, ethics, the criteria used for decision making, personal philosophy, hopes and dreams, and values and personal integrity. Given the choice between two equally competent persons, I would vote for the person of faith over the one without faith. Churches are not permitted to endorse particular candidates; this regulation is not a matter of constitutional law, but is implemented through IRS rules governing tax-exempt groups.

23

Having noted that faith is important in choosing elected officials, we should acknowledge that a candidate's faith is not the only qualification we need to consider as informed voters. Not all persons who are faithful Christians necessarily have the skills and experience to hold office. The best candidate for office must have competence, experience, personal integrity, keen intelligence, a good heart, a talent for relating to people, the ability to communicate, and a host of other qualifications. The best candidate may not be a Christian. Furthermore, some politicians have become quite adept at using the church by putting on the pretense of having a deep faith—a faith that seems to disappear once the candidate is elected to office. All of which points to the challenge of actually knowing how genuine a candidate's faith truly is. Yet I still maintain that if two candidates are equally qualified, I would choose the candidate who will seek to do what is right in all circumstances, especially because he or she sees public service as an opportunity to serve God as well as neighbor.

The second, and more critical section of the Constitution when it comes to the relationship between church and state is the First Amendment to the Constitution which reads, "Congress shall make no law respecting an establishment of religion, or prohibiting the free exercise thereof; or abridging the freedom of speech, or of the press; or the right of the people peaceably to assemble, and to petition the government for a redress of grievances."

The religious issue was the very first item in a list of the most important and valued rights of the people of this new republic. This amendment is fairly simple; its purpose is to make clear that the United States would not follow the model of the European states where the established state church had a powerful influence over the government. Our founders wanted to ensure that no one church would receive the endorsement of the nation. No one sect would have power over the others. The Pilgrims who landed at Plymouth Rock were coming to a new country to gain this freedom. It is part of what we treasure in this country of ours.

In addition, Congress could not prohibit the exercise of religion. The government would not be linked with a particular religious group and would not be involved in regulating religion. The Constitution does not use the phrase "separation of church and state"—Thomas Jefferson first coined this phrase in 1801 to describe his understanding of the First Amendment—but it was clear that there was to be no direct link between church and state.

This was a very, very good thing. In the last two hundred years the official relationship of the church with the state in some countries has resulted in a practice of Christianity that is weak. Families may still want their children baptized and confirmed, but church attendance and participation in church-related activities is low. The society becomes more and more oriented toward secular interests. The experience of countries with established churches seems to indicate that every time the state gets involved in religion, religion ultimately loses. The church loses its voice and its vitality in countries where there is a strong link between the state and a particular church. The state too often uses religion as a tool, and the church loses its nerve in speaking up against the state, as was the case with the official state church in South Africa for many decades and also the case with the state churches in Nazi Germany.

Clearly the state should not try to do the work of the church, and churches have no business asking the state to do so. *But the church can be involved in influencing the state; the church can work for better policies; the church does have an obligation to speak out and address justice and morality issues.*

The state and the church should not take on an antagonistic stance toward each other; they need each other. Our nation was founded with a positive view of religion, which was understood to be a vital part of our nation and our culture Without it the republic was given little chance of succeeding.

Forging a New Relationship
Between Church and State

The church needs the state. It needs the state to be the authority that governs justly, works for the common good, protects the interests and rights of all people, and works for justice on a global level. The church needs the state for order, justice, and the protection of basic civil liberties.

But the state needs the church as well. *The state needs the church to shape the values, ethics, hopes, worldview, and dreams of the culture.* Religion is the single most powerful influence in shaping these values and hopes and the greatest source of our highest ideals. The state develops laws based upon the values of the people. When the church fails at its task, the state pays the price in a populace with lowered moral vision, greater crime, greater social problems, and a reduced clarity in differentiating between right and wrong.

In a conversation with an FBI agent last year, I learned that the bureau faces an increasing challenge in getting white-collar crime convictions in court. The values of the populace have declined to a point where many folks in a jury of peers no longer clearly see the distinction between right and wrong. The state, at every level, needs the church to do its work of forming persons who have a strong moral vision.

The state needs the church to think through the tough and challenging ethical issues, to bring clarity, and to shape the common moral vision based upon the ultimate concerns that are shared in the faith community. The state cannot impose ultimate concerns or establish our values, for it relies on common consent and has no underlying basis of its own for making moral judgments. But the people can incorporate the moral discernment learned in the community of faith into our shared sense of right and wrong, and can, through legislative means, seek to codify this moral vision. The church's leadership will be especially important in the future when it comes to the complex bioethical issues we will face.

The state needs the church to produce capable leaders with a deep faith and the highest personal integrity, along with an altruistic sense of calling, to public service. Too often those who aspire to the highest public offices have struggled with the conflict between their altruistic calling and their driven ego. The state is in dire need of officeholders who understand that public service is an important calling. My hope is that many of you reading this book will consider how God might use you to shape our world through the area of public service. Christians need to get involved in the political process. A governor, a legislator, a city council representative, a Supreme Court justice, and even a president could come from your congregation. But if you get involved in the political process, do so with the highest of motives and the desire to please and honor God as you do. Live your faith in your relationships and demonstrate it in how you get elected.

Finally, *the state needs the church to take seriously the biblical command to pray for our leaders.* I am weary of hearing Christians, including pastors, denigrating political leaders. Political leaders are people, people who need our prayers, our input, our encouragement, not our verbal attacks, insults, and rancor. If Christ calls us to love our neighbor—and even our enemy—how much more so our politicians, whether we agree with them or not. This was the very point the apostle Paul was making when he wrote to Titus, "Remind them to be subject to rulers and authorities, to be obedient, to be ready for every good work, to speak evil of no one, to avoid quarreling, to be gentle, and to show every courtesy to everyone" (Titus 3:1–2).

Two Controversial Issues and One Possible Christian Response

I will offer two concrete examples of controversial church and state issues that have been in the news—stories in which I believe the church, and individual Christians, were fighting the wrong battles.

The first story comes from the town of Florissant, Missouri. In this town at Christmastime a nativity scene is erected on public property. This display was recently challenged in court and its legality was upheld by the United States Court of Appeals for the Eighth Circuit because the nativity scene was one part of a large array of holiday symbols, some of them clearly nonreligious. In other words, the court ruled that the manger could be displayed as long as it was given no more prominence than Rudolph the Red-Nosed Reindeer and Santa Claus. Many religious leaders celebrated this ruling that allowed the nativity scene on city property. But when I read of this "victory" for the Christians in Florissant, I wondered if this is really a victory indeed. Does the church really want the story of the birth of Christ laid out alongside of Rudolph the Red-Nosed Reindeer and Frosty the Snowman? Does this in any way diminish our story—placing it in the same category as these other holiday themes? Do we really want the Christ Child displayed among candy canes and reindeer? I believe that the nativity is the church's story. It is our job to tell the story in creative new ways. But I do fear when the state appropriates our story, even if with the best of motives. Will the story retain its life-changing power? And finally, when the nonreligious look at cases like this, does our attitude, our displays, and our booths draw the lost to Christ, or turn them away? If people are going to hear the Christmas story, it won't be because we let municipalities do the job of telling the story for us, it will be because *we* go out to where the people are and *we* tell the story. We've got to the be ones shouting, "This isn't simply the 'holiday season'—this is Christmas!" We need to be inviting people to experience the birth of the Christ Child here—in the church!

The second example from the news that touches on this issue is the controversy over prayers at official state functions. The opening prayer or invocation given at the Kansas state legislature in my home state is one example. The hoopla over this issue has revolved around certain pastors who use the prayer as an opportunity to preach, and others who end their prayers with "in Jesus' name." This may be fine if you were speaking in a church to a gathering of Christians, but in the legislature there are people from different religious backgrounds. I have given the opening invocation at the state legislature as well as the prayer at the inauguration of Kansas Governor Bill Graves in 1999. I often pray at events where there are interfaith audiences. I am certain that if I have been invited to pray for a group that includes non-Christians and I am praying at the group's behest, then my prayer must be for everyone in the group, and not just for the Christians.

When we pray to God, God hears our prayer, whether we have ended it with "in Jesus' name" or not. My personal prayers and my pastoral prayers in my congregation will end in this biblical way. But when praying with and for interfaith groups, I am not making a positive witness for Christ by praying in a way that is hurtful to non-Christians. In fact, quite the opposite. Witnessing for Christ won't happen by trying to turn the state into a tool for evangelism.

Jesus was clear, we are to be in the world but not of it. We are to view our lives as pilgrims, or in the words of theologians and ethicists Stanley Hauerwas and William Willimon, as "resident aliens." And yet we live in a democratic nation where a majority of people are Christians. We have the opportunity to be catalysts shaping our culture as salt and light. We have the right to influence what happens in our country for the common good. We should not try to use the government to promote our faith—our government agencies have a tough enough time doing everything else they are asked to do, and I am not sure we would like the results! But we must think through controversial issues, prayerfully discerning God's will for our lives. I hope in the next six chapters, even when you disagree with my conclusions, you will take seriously the need for Christian people to wrestle with these issues and that you will seek to let your light so shine before others that they will see your good works and give glory to your Father who is in heaven.

29

Questions for Reflection

1. Read Luke 20:20–25. What issues do these verses raise about the relationship of church and state? What things do you think Jesus intends to include in the phrase "the things that are the emperor's"? What is included in the phrase "the things that are God's"? Does Caesar belong to God?

2. Read the words to the hymn "This Is My Song" by Lloyd Stone and Georgia Harkness (*United Methodist Hymnal* [Nashville: The United Methodist Publishing House, 1989], #437). What hopes for our country are expressed in this song? What hopes for other nations? What values and concerns that are voiced in this song do we have in common with people of other religious faiths? What does the song pray for that is specifically Christian?

3. Inside the Liberty Bell in Philadelphia are engraved words from the Bible: "Proclaim LIBERTY throughout all the land" (see Leviticus 25:10). Do you think having a Bible verse on a national symbol violates the separation of church and state? What do you think these words meant to those who founded our nation in the eighteenth century? Look at the proclamations for the Jubilee Year in Leviticus 25 and discuss what "proclaim liberty" meant to the Hebrew people in the time of Moses. What does it mean to modern Americans?

4. John Wesley raised issues in his time that were considered to be none of the church's business. He was especially concerned about slavery and about the poverty and inhumane conditions brought about by the industrial revolution. Though he remained an Anglican priest, he worked at these issues outside the structures of the Church of England, resulting in the movement that became the Methodist Church. Discuss why it would be difficult to call for government reforms from within the state church. What issues in today's culture might Wesley address? What difficulties do mainline denominations experience in trying to be our society's conscience? How do you think Wesley balanced his political concerns with his dedication to

the spiritual disciplines of prayer, public worship, and Bible study?

5. What examples of the church's struggle to change the values of the state can you think of? One topic for study and discussion might be the role of the Confessing Church in Nazi Germany. Reading a short biography of Dietrich Bonhoeffer and some of his writings such as *Letters and Papers from Prison* could be part of this project.

6. Write a prayer for our country and for the courage of the church to speak out. Ask for suggestions from others in the congregation, including children, as to what concerns should be included and what leaders should be prayed for.

Who was with you, O God of awesome majesty, when you laid the foundation of the earth and all the morning stars sang together? Forgive us our arrogance. Teach us the persistence of Job, who waited through your silence and heard your mighty voice. Teach us the openness of a child at school that we may know your world in the vastness of its mystery. Teach us the songs of the poets that we may find words to praise your name: "The heavens tell your glory and the firmament proclaims your handiwork." We thank you, O God, that Christ your Word was with you at the beginning and, through the gift of your Spirit, is with us now to show us your way, your truth, your life. In his name we pray; Amen.

CHAPTER TWO

Creation and Evolution in the Public Schools

In the beginning when God created the heavens and
the earth, the earth was a formless void and darkness
covered the face of the deep, while a wind from God
swept over the face of the waters. Then God said, "Let
there be light"; and there was light. And God saw that
the light was good; and God separated the light from
the darkness. God called the light Day, and the darkness he called Night. And there was evening and there
was morning, the first day. (Genesis 1:1-5)

✽   ✽   ✽   ✽   ✽

Those of us who live in Kansas have a special interest in
the controversy surrounding the teaching of the theory of
evolution in public schools. In a much publicized 1999 decision
the Kansas State Board of Education voted to eliminate questions about evolution in statewide testing of public school
students. Biology teachers were not forbidden to teach about
evolution, but because it would not appear on state-sanctioned
standardized tests, many were expected to treat it lightly or
skip over it entirely in the classroom. The *Kansas City Star*
called the decision a blunder, and parents were concerned that
Kansas students would not measure up in science when they
compete with students from other states for college placement.

The governor of Kansas was alarmed by the amount of negative and even derisive reaction to the decision from outside the state, and in a television interview remarked that many people wanted to know "What is going on in the state of Kansas?"

What *is* going on in Kansas? You may not live in Kansas, but there is likely a large number of people in your state who would like to effect the same change in your school board that took place in the Sunflower State. In this chapter we will examine the issues surrounding evolution and how thinking Christians might approach this fascinating issue.

Before launching into this chapter it is important for you to know what research went into my study. I began by reading parts of Darwin's *The Origin of Species* (London: Oxford University Press, 1998). I also read the sections on evolution from the textbooks in biology used at our local high school and community college. I read portions of the National Academy of Sciences' book *Teaching About Evolution and the Nature of Science* (Washington, D.C.: National Academy Press, 1998), prepared specifically to counter the claims of the opponents of teaching evolution. In addition I have read numerous articles drawn from the Internet in support of teaching evolution.

On the opposite side of the debate, I have read Hank Hanegraaff's *The Face that Demonstrates the Farce of Evolution* (Nashville: Word, 1998) and Jonathan Sarfati's *Refuting Evolution* (Colorado Springs: Master Books, 1999), written in response to the National Academy of Sciences' book. In addition I have read numerous sections of Philip Johnson's *Darwin on Trial* (Downers Grove, Ill.: InterVarsity Press, 1993) and Gerald Schroeder's *The Science of God* (New York: Broadway Books, 1998). Numerous articles and interviews taken from the Internet, including those from the Institute for Creation Research were a part of my studies. Finally, I was able to read the minutes from the Kansas State Board of Education meeting where the final science standards were voted on and the official Kansas Curricular Standards for Science Education were adopted in December 1999.

34

Before examining the merit of evolution's claims, let's take a look at the biblical account of creation as found in Genesis, to see if evolutionary theory can in any way be reconciled with the Scriptures. To help us understand why this remains such a controversial issue, we need to understand the four primary ways of approaching the Genesis account of creation.

Four Approaches to the Genesis Account of Creation

Let's begin with what was the dominant approach to the creation account for nearly three thousand years. The contemporary supporters of this approach are best described as "young-earth biblical literalists." Among the leading proponents of this view today are the folks at the Institute for Creation Research in Santee, California.

According to proponents of this theory, Genesis 1 accurately represents the basic facts surrounding creation. Creation took place in six twenty-four-hour days, in the order in which it is represented in Genesis. Later, a universal flood—described in the story of Noah and the ark—took place, and water covered the entire planet. A sum of years calculated using the genealogies of the Old Testament is taken to be the actual age of the planet and the period of time since the beginning of the universe. Using this information they propose that the universe, and our planet, is less than ten thousand years old. Dinosaurs and humans walked the planet at the same time, but like many other animals, dinosaurs are simply not mentioned by name in the Genesis story. The flood is the likely explanation for the demise of the dinosaurs, and the pressure created by the weight of the flood waters was the primary force in creating fossils. These views represent what is usually meant by the term *creation science.* I struggle to find this argument compelling, and I believe this view is based upon a faulty understanding of the Genesis account of creation.

35

The second group, with which I am somewhat more sympathetic, are the "old-earth biblical literalists." They believe the Genesis account must be taken literally and that when the Bible speaks about scientific matters it is always correct, but they leave a bit of wiggle room. They note that the Scriptures teach: "With the Lord one day is like a thousand years, and a thousand years are like one day" (2 Peter 3:8). They believe each day described in Genesis 1 could be a period or an epoch spanning millions and millions of years. They tend to accept the dating of scientists who say that the earth could be as old as 4.6 billion years.

Some of them also offer another interesting idea that helps open the door to issues such as when the dinosaurs lived and how the fossil record came to be. They point to Genesis 1:1–2, and see between these two verses the possibility of a vast period of time during which, perhaps, cataclysmic events took place. First, God creates the heavens and the earth, and then, in this gap, there is room for God's creative work with dinosaurs and all kinds of creatures. But notice, in verse 2, the earth is now covered in darkness and water, perhaps the result of an asteroid hitting the earth as has been proposed as a reason for the demise of the dinosaurs. Verse three is then the re-creation of the planet. Proponents of this last idea call this the "gap theory."

Let us look briefly now at the third view, the "naturalistic and mythological" approach to the Genesis story, which is at the other end of the spectrum from "creation science." These thinkers believe that the Genesis story of creation is just that—a story with little credibility for the modern era. They see it as a myth for prescientific people who needed the concept of God to explain what they could not understand. Those who hold this position believe that evolutionary theory alone is sufficient to explain all that exists. The dismissing of the Genesis account of creation in this way is not acceptable to most Christians.

Finally, there is an approach to Genesis that I will call the "biblical-scientific synthesis" approach. This is the approach held by many scientists and biblical scholars and the one that nearly every mainline Protestant denomination, as well as the

Roman Catholic Church and even many evangelical churches, take. This view begins by recognizing what Genesis 1–3 *is* meant to teach and what it *is not* meant to teach. These verses are clearly meant to lay claim to the *fact* that God is the creator of everything. Nothing exists apart from God's creative word, will, and power. The Genesis account teaches us God is the rightful ruler of all things, owner of all things, and that all things are a reflection of the Creator. These verses are meant to teach that everything God designed is good, that God created everything out of love for us and a desire to give God's own self to us. The Genesis creation poem was intended to make clear to the ancient Israelites, living in the midst of peoples who worshiped the sun, moon, stars, animals, and inanimate objects that none of these things are gods. Israel's God, in fact, created them all!

But listen carefully: These verses were not meant to teach us the *how* and the *when* of creation, only the *Who* and the *why*! This section of Genesis is set in poetic language, the language of faith, not science. This does not mean that the poetry of Genesis stands counter to scientific discoveries but that it serves a higher purpose, leading us to the truth about God our Creator and our relationship to God. The creation poem is meant to communicate the purposes of life. It is meant to describe in epic fashion the most marvelous theological truth of all: that Israel's God was not merely another regional god like the other nations served but is, in fact, the LORD God who, by God's very words, called forth light from darkness and life from nothing at all!

This story was not meant to be read with a kind of hyperliteralism; it was intended instead to be read and taken seriously as a statement of faith in God. The word *Adam* was a symbolic name; it meant "man" and the name *Eve* meant "woman." As you may know, there are actually two creation accounts found in Genesis: the first in chapter one and the second beginning with chapter two, verse four. Even the order given for the creation of some things varies between these two accounts, which were collected and brought together in Gene-

37

sis by an ancient Israelite author. God has indeed inspired these words; make no mistake about it. But God's words are meant to assure the prescientific people, as well as modern people, of the fact that God is the Creator. With this assurance guiding us, we can freely engage in scientific research, using the intelligence and diligence that God has given us, and we can be open to new discoveries.

It is obvious that the original audience of Genesis could not possibly have understood protons and DNA structure; what they needed to know thirty-two hundred years ago was that God created everything and God has a plan and purpose for us and all creation. God was working to bring all created things into being but found it unnecessary to reveal the details of how it was accomplished. God gives us the joy and privilege as human beings to unravel some of the mysteries of the "how" of creation, but all our discoveries will never dismiss the need for God. Instead we will continue to be amazed at what God did and marvel at God's majesty.

What amazes me about the biblical account is that though it was written over thirty-two hundred years before the big bang theory was posited, it captures the essence of this theory. Both the Bible and science agree that the universe had a beginning point. They agree that first there was nothing, and then there was light, and from this beginning, all the galaxies of the universe were formed. Three millennia before scientists told us that the earth would have been formless and void for nearly a billion years before life began to appear, the prescientific story of Genesis suggested this occurrence. Thirty-two centuries before Darwin proposed that life began in the seas, the author of Genesis told us that the first creatures God brought forth were in the seas, when God said, "Let the waters bring forth swarms of living creatures" (Genesis 1:20). And three thousand years before chemists helped us understand that even human beings come from the same carbon compounds found in the earth, the writer of Genesis told us that God took the dust of the earth and shaped it into a human being and breathed into it the breath of life. Genesis is a poetic, powerful, and majestic way of revealing not the processes of creation but the fact that God did these things.

Those who hold this view are not threatened by science exploring the "how" of creation. At every stage we step back and evaluate the scientists' theories and discoveries, and they only serve to heighten the sense of awe at a God who designed all creation!

Evolution—What's All the Fuss About?

So what is all the fuss about? Most of us, I expect, would say that at least some aspects of the theory of evolution make sense and help us understand the processes of life. Some, however, still maintain that it doesn't make sense at all and see it as a threat to our faith.

In many ways what we are seeing today with regard to evolution in the schools is a repeat of the excitement and upheaval surrounding the Scopes trial of 1925 when the teaching of evolution was first put on trial. John T. Scopes was tried for violating Tennessee state law by teaching the theory of evolution in his public school classroom. The trial attracted national attention, and the two sides engaged in highly emotional debate on the street and in the media. There was no middle ground: One side was characterized as believing that human beings are descended from apes—a misrepresentation of Darwin's views in any case—and the other side was thought to be naive, unscientific, and antiprogress because they were unable to move beyond the details of the Genesis account in a strict, literal sense as the final word on how God created life. The two most famous lawyers of the day came to Dayton, Tennessee, to argue the case: William Jennings Bryan representing the state and Clarence Darrow representing Scopes. In many ways the arguments these two attorneys presented are still the primary arguments offered by each side in the great debate today.

Let's take a closer look at evolution. Evolution is, at core, the predominant scientific theory meant to answer the following questions: What is the origin of all life forms on our planet? Why is there such diversity among living creatures? And, how do we explain the commonality among all living things? Evolution explains the commonality and diversity of all living things by means of a process of change shaped by random mutation, adaptation, and survival of the fittest. The emphasis on survival places a premium on mating and reproduction. We may well worry that such a mechanistic view of life is in danger of leaving out the spiritual dimension entirely, but certain thinkers find the concept of quantifiable and predictable changes to be liberating.

Darwin's book, *The Origin of Species,* was first published in 1859 but drew upon other works published before it. He proposed that all life forms today originated from a few—or perhaps even one—common ancestors, thus explaining some of the fundamental commonality among all living things. That original microorganism reproduced, and its offspring would occasionally undergo random mutations that resulted in small changes in the life form. Some of these changes were deadly, but some were positive. The mutated cells were enabled to reproduce more effectively, giving rise to variation. From here Darwin took a bigger leap and said that, given billions of years, and millions of these changes, whole new and complex life forms would arise and go through the same process, producing families of organisms which, as they became increasingly different from one another became individual species. And through this process, Darwin believed we could account for all life forms as we know them, including you and me.

The implications of this theory were considered to be profound, not merely for science but for philosophy, sociology, psychology, and nearly every other discipline. For some thinkers, the theory offered an explanation of life without the need for God. Some of Darwin's followers felt that the logical consequence of the theory was the belief that life was simply the result of chance. *There is no meaning, no purpose, no order, and no plan to life as we know it—all is chance.* Survival and reproduction are the ultimate goals of life. And being the fittest, defined by those most able to acquire food, safety, and mates, is the means to accomplishing life's goals.

Some followers of Darwin misused the theory of evolution as a means of reinforcing racist ideas, always believing that the most evolved human beings were those who looked most like themselves. Hitler's philosophy was shaped by these views, and he claimed they offered justification for his plans to exterminate what he considered to be inferior races.

For others this theory was liberating, setting them free from the what they believed were outmoded concepts of divine law. Evolution could grant them permission to pursue their own lifestyles without guilt because now there was no ultimate right or wrong; conscience was merely fashioned by one's family and culture. If there was no meaning to life, there was also no ultimate judgment day. Karl Marx believed it offered a good foundation for his *Communist Manifesto* and asked Darwin for permission to dedicate this work to the biologist. (Darwin refused.) The misuse of Darwin's views does not point to the inaccuracy of evolutionary concepts, per se, only to the critical reason why evolution, divorced from any concept of God, is a woefully inadequate foundation for a philosophy of life.

As an illustration of the complexity of the life processes we are talking about, recall observing an amoeba through a microscope. An amoeba is among the simplest life forms; it is a single-cell organism. Yet as simple as it is, it is still an amazing creature. It has a cell wall. It has a digestive system. It has an engine that converts food to energy. It has a propulsion system and a pressurization system. It can divide and multiply. It produces waste, and it has its own genetic software. This is a living machine—it is beautiful. But here is where I begin to struggle with evolution a bit. Our brightest and best scientists cannot create amoebas. They are so complex that we who can send people to outer space cannot create one little amoeba. We

41

know the basic ingredients. We understand how an amoeba works. But that's about as far as it goes!

Now, here's why evolution without God doesn't work for me. Evolutionary theory implies that what we can't do, as intelligent as we are, with all our knowledge and abilities, happened on its own. A little of this base ingredient, a little of that one. A little lightning. A bit of water. And then, about a billion years—and finally, our wonderful friend was born! No designer. No one to write the software for it. A living entity so complex we can't make one was spontaneously generated in the primordial soup. And then, this entity was born with instructions for reproducing! That, to me, is unfathomable!

But let's just say our little friend the amoeba was born in this way. Do you have any clue how much more complicated you are than this little guy? It took teams of scientists twelve years just to try to unravel your genetic coding. In some very small way this would be like my taking the components of silica, plastic, and metal, putting them in a box and shaking, in hopes that one day a laptop computer would come out. How long would I need to shake until it happened? It would never happen! And yet you are much more complex than a computer!

Many pastors, including myself, do not dismiss the concepts and basic principles of evolution. I think that Darwin's theories help us make sense of many things—and I accept much of evolutionary theory as the best plausible explanation of the development of the various forms of life and the extinction of others. We can observe evolutionary principles at work in the gradual adaptation of bacteria so that they can resist certain antibiotics, for example. But even in these cases evolution offers only a limited explanation; evolutionary theory alone is not enough to explain the fact of life as we know it.

In our first chapter we noted that to God there is no distinction between sacred and secular. Everything belongs to God and God rules over all. Likewise, there is no distinction for God between supernatural and naturalistic. This is a false dichotomy. God designs the biological processes, provides the energy that makes them go, writes the software code that is played out in cell division and the development of life, pre-wires cells for mutations—which may be far less random than we might think—and breathes on certain species, calling forth some from others. This is part of God's handiwork! The concept of evolution has never kept me from marveling at the wonders of God's creation, nor from loving and giving praise to God as our Creator. Evolution, taught with ample humility, is no danger to the faith of our children.

Yet I think science textbooks are remiss in not, at the very least, including a word about the fact that a vast majority of people believe that evolution alone cannot explain the marvels and wonders of life. For these people, the concept of an Intelligent Designer is a critical part of being able to accept evolution. I believe this concept could be expressed very candidly, without either pushing the idea, or ridiculing it. A statement that recognizes the gaps in evolutionary theory and allows for the possibility of believing in the work of a Creator who works alongside evolution could be worded very positively, without either supporting or denying the statement. One or two lines in the textbooks would go a long way toward recognizing what is philosophically consistent with the understanding and beliefs of a vast majority of people, including a large number of scientists—namely, that evolution alone seems inadequate in explaining the amazing development of life. I find it academically dishonest not to include a statement that acknowledges the possibility of the work of a Supreme Being at the beginning of creation and throughout the evolutionary process.

I believe that it was the intention on the part of some members of the Kansas State Board of Education to recognize the need for an acknowledgment of the Creator's role in a way similar to what I've just suggested. But I believe they went too far and took the wrong approach. In reading the minutes of their meeting, I can only conclude that they did not follow through as carefully as they should have on the revision proposed by a three-member study committee. In addition, by removing evolution from testing they made the teaching of it nearly optional. Those teachers who do not believe in any aspects of evolutionary theory will find it easy to leave this subject out of their instruction. As a result some students might come through the Kansas education system with gaps in their knowledge of modern science. This outcome is disappointing and doesn't solve the problem. I want my children to learn the dominant theories in biology. But I would also like them to read in their textbooks that not everyone finds evolution *alone* to be a satisfactory solution to the question of human origins.

The Real Point of Genesis

This topic is important to wrestle with. But more important is the real point of the creation story. It was not meant to teach us *how* God created, but *that* God created. Creation is a gift to us. And all of creation is a reflection of the wonder of the Creator. God's creation—from the amoeba, to the newborn child, to the wonders of the galaxies and stars—points to the majesty of the God who caused the big bang, who called forth the light and darkness, who spoke and the waters swarmed with life, and who created you in God's own image. You are no accident: You were designed by God to be recipients of God's love and to enjoy creation, to walk with God, know God, and do God's will. And this Creator is not some anonymous Intelligent Designer. No. God is the one who has been revealed by becoming one of us in Jesus Christ. There is no greater joy, no greater life, than knowing and following God.

The Christian gospel teaches that before the big bang, God was. All creation is the handiwork of God—a reflection of God's beauty, power, and majesty. It never tries to tell us how God created. Over the 4.5 billion years of life on this planet God no doubt worked through processes and experimentation, experiencing the joy of designing and creating the myriad of life forms that have existed on earth during its history. As the crowning act of God's creative work, God brought forth, perhaps from prior forms of life, the first human beings.

44

Different from any creatures that had come before them—for these were created in God's own image—they possessed a soul, an ability to think, understand, love, and worship. Humanity, according to the Christian faith, was no mere accident, not simply the latest example of a random mutation. No, we were fashioned by the Creator, in God's own image. The apostle Paul notes in Ephesians 2:10 that we are God's *poema*, the Greek word from which our English word *poem* is derived. We are God's poetry, God's works of art!

Evolution is not the enemy of Christian faith; it is merely a way of talking about one possible process God used to develop the wonders of life on our planet. But evolution alone, without God, seems ill equipped to explain the origin of life or the magnificence of the human spirit. Science can and will help us understand how things work. The creation story of Genesis was never meant to teach us this. Instead, it was meant to teach us that behind all of these "hows" of creation, lies the ultimate "Who" of creation: the God who designed the systems and processes, who set them all in motion, and of whose beauty, power, and love all creation is merely a reflection.

A final word of postscript: The Kansas State Board of Education has since reversed its earlier decision and has reinstated testing requirements related to the theory of evolution.

❋   ❋   ❋   ❋   ❋

Questions for Reflection

1. What do you think are the advantages of reading Genesis 1:1–31 as poetry? What are the difficulties of poetry as a literary form? Write these images on a chalkboard or newsprint and talk about what they suggest: "formless void" (v. 2), "wind" (v. 2), "dome" (vv. 6–8), "waters...gathered together" (vv. 9–10), "lights...to separate the day from the night" (v. 14), "be fruitful" (v. 22), "in our image" (v. 26), and "God blessed them" (v. 28). What does it mean for humans to have "dominion" over the animals (v. 26)?

2. Read John 1:1–5. As in Genesis 1 these verses are a statement of faith in poetic form, affirming not only that God was responsible for all creation but also that Christ was with God at the beginning. Read aloud verses 3–4. Does "life" have more than the obvious meaning here and in other places in the Gospels? What variations of meaning can you see in these terms: "abundant life," "eternal life," "newness of life," and "life from above"? What is new about the life we receive at our baptism (see Romans 6:1–11)?

3. Read Revelation 21:1–7. What is new about the "new creation"? What images come to mind from the phrase "the spring of the water of life"? What does it mean that God is "the beginning and the end"? What does this assurance promise us?

4. Look up the Affirmations of Faith in the *United Methodist Hymnal* (Nashville: The United Methodist Publishing House, 1989, #880–89). Which ones include a statement of belief about God's act of creating? What variations do you notice in the ways this belief is expressed? Also using the hymnal, find hymns listed under "Creation" (see the "Index of Topics and Categories") and choose one to sing.

5. Working together with others and, if possible, consulting with a science teacher, write a proposal for a statement that could be included in a textbook to acknowledge the possibility of a Divine Creator, not to replace the teaching of evolutionary theory but to recognize its limits. Keep in mind the precepts of the separation of church and state and the sensitivities and rights of the nonbelievers who will use this book.

6. Watch a video of the movie *Inherit the Wind*, a fictionalized account of the Scopes trial, or read the play as a group and discuss the issues raised by it. How have attitudes about the Bible and science changed since 1925?

7. Write a responsive prayer that invites participants to offer praise and thanks to God our Creator. After each individual petition or thanksgiving, the group offers a response in unison such as "And God saw that it was good."

God of life, we know you through the gift of your Son, Jesus Christ our Lord, who died on the cross that we might live. Teach us to long for your justice and to bring the goodness of your life-giving love to all we encounter. Through your grace alone, we are made worthy to live in your presence; may we extend your embrace to those who, like your Son, are despised and rejected. Your mercy falls down on the just and on the unjust like rain from heaven; grant us the courage to be merciful in your name. We ask these things for the sake of your Son, Jesus our Savior; Amen.

CHAPTER THREE

The Death Penalty

For your own lifeblood I will surely require a reckoning: from every animal I will require it and from human beings, each one for the blood of another, I will require a reckoning for human life.
Whoever sheds the blood of a human,
    by a human shall that person's blood be shed;
for in his own image
    God made humankind. (Genesis 9:5–6)

"You have heard that it was said, 'An eye for an eye and a tooth for a tooth.' But I say to you, Do not resist an evildoer. But if anyone strikes you on the right cheek, turn the other also; and if anyone wants to sue you and take your coat, give your cloak as well; and if anyone forces you to go one mile, go also the second mile." (Matthew 5:38–41)

I am grateful to Christ Jesus our Lord, who has strengthened me, because he judged me faithful and appointed me to his service, even though I was formerly a blasphemer, a persecutor, and a man of violence. But I received mercy because I had acted ignorantly in unbelief, and the grace of our Lord overflowed for me with the faith and love that are in Christ Jesus. The saying is sure and worthy of full acceptance, that Christ Jesus came into the world to save sinners—of whom I am the foremost. But for that very reason I received mercy, so that in me, as the foremost, Jesus Christ might display the utmost patience, making me an example to those who would come to believe in him for eternal life. (1 Timothy 1:12–16)

❄   ❄   ❄   ❄   ❄

Why are we talking about the death penalty in the church? That's the question some of you are asking as we continue our series on controversial issues. Sometimes people tell me that they wish we would not discuss topics like this one in church or that they wish I would not preach on them. "We just need to talk about the Bible and God," they say. But is it really that simple? Many of my sermons are on overtly spiritual topics—sermons about the life of Jesus or prayer or the habits of highly effective Christians. But shouldn't our faith have something to say to the really serious moral and ethical issues that concern our nation? What we believe about God and our understanding of the Bible should influence the way we face difficult challenges as individuals and as a society.

In our country the death penalty is an increasingly urgent topic. The United States is executing more people at the present time than at any other time in our past. We cannot possibly think as Christians that God has nothing to say to us about this issue. Does God care whether we put to death those who have committed horrible crimes? Surely God does have a view on this issue. As Christians, our aim must be to seek to discern God's will and to align our views and opinions with God's perspective.

Furthermore, it is imperative that Christians offer help in thinking through this issue for society as a whole. Even those in the legal and criminal justice field look to the church and religious thinkers for help in wrestling with these important issues. "American Justice," a program shown on the Arts and Entertainment Network, noted that there are twenty-five hundred men and women on death row in the United States, and concern is growing about the increasing rate at which the state is carrying out executions. The program's host asked pointedly if our justice system has the means or the capability to deal with the host of moral and philosophical questions surrounding the issue of the state's taking of human lives. As Christians, I think we must conclude that the state cannot possibly deal with all these questions. Yet executions are done by the state in our name as citizens. We must therefore ask who makes the decisions for us concerning the death penalty and what is the basis for these decisions.

We noted earlier that laws are derived from the culture, and the culture's views are shaped by something. As Christians, our aim should be to shape our culture. Our responsibility is to look to the Bible, the Christian tradition, our experience of the Holy Spirit, and our God-given reason to try to discern God's will concerning our country's laws regarding the death penalty. But it is not always easy to discern God's will. The Bible can be used to support both sides of this debate, and few thinking people do not struggle with this issue. I will admit that I struggle with both sides of this debate and have found myself wavering both for and against the death penalty at various times in my life. My hope is to offer you the case on both sides, to bring some degree of theological reflection to the issue, and then invite you to wrestle with your own position as to whether the state should put convicted criminals to death.

The Old Testament and the Death Penalty

We begin our study of the death penalty by looking to the Law of Moses. In Genesis 9:5-6 we find an ancient tradition regarding murder, a tradition that predates Moses by hundreds of years and one that is consistent with other ancient law codes of the Near East. This passage takes us back to the time of Noah, following the Flood. God has for the first time given human beings permission to kill and eat animals, but they are not to kill other humans. The reason: Human beings are created in the image of God. God's spirit has been breathed into us. We are each created by God, therefore no one but God has the authority to take another's life. So, in this passage God gives to the people the command: If a human murders another human, by a human hand the murderer too shall die. The passage clearly supports the death penalty concept; it was meant to deter persons from murdering.

Numbers 35:16–21 also supports the death penalty. These verses specify that if a death results from someone striking another with an iron or wood object or a stone, or if a death occurs when two people are wrestling or hitting with fists, the perpetrator shall surely be put to death. Even here the distinction between manslaughter and murder is noted; the law imposes the death penalty on murderers but makes provision for those who accidentally kill another. Lacking a legal justice system as we know it, the victim's family was allowed to appoint a family member as an "avenger of blood," who, upon the testimony of two witnesses, put the murderer to death. It is important to note that the purpose of these laws was to deter people from killing one another. Throughout the Old Testament times, we find the death penalty was supported and used as a means of justice. But it is important to note that the reason murder was taken so seriously by the ancient Hebrews was that their faith taught them that each human life is valued by God. And God alone claims the right to end a human life.

Before we determine that the Bible unequivocally supports the death penalty, it is important that we understand a bit more about the Old Testament, the reasons behind the death penalty in the Old Testament, and the situations in which it was applied.

There are five things to note about the death penalty in the Old Testament: The first is the key role it played in maintaining social order. The legal code found in Exodus, Leviticus, and Deuteronomy had its origins in the Mosaic period when Israel wandered in the wilderness as a nomadic people. The use of the death penalty was a means of maintaining order in a society with no criminal justice system, no police force, and no prisons. Judges heard cases and made judgments based on the testimony of two witnesses, but beyond that there was no adequate formal structure for maintaining order. In such an environment the death penalty provided a serious deterrent, and it served its purpose of eliminating both lawlessness and unfaithfulness to God and others. It was quite effective; police were not needed. An individual could make a claim about another and could file charges with the priest or the judge. Once a conviction was pronounced by the judge, the sentence was carried out by the offended party, an avenger acting in the victim's name, or representatives of the community.

Generally executions took place by stoning, though the law provided for other means of administering capital punishment as well. Note that since the death penalty was the primary means of maintaining order, it was prescribed for a host of different sins; eleven crimes in all were punishable by death. These included disobedience of or disrespect toward one's parents, violating the Sabbath by working on Saturday, and sexual activity outside of marriage. Few of those who point to the Old Testament as justification for the death penalty would be willing to accept the death penalty as it is presented there. It is hard to be certain, but I have a hunch that few of you reading these words would still be alive today if we applied the death penalty to those who disobeyed parents or who failed to attend worship or who worked on a Sunday.

The death penalty, as it related to murder charges, was intended to make a specific point—that life is sacred and that God is the only rightful taker of life. To murder is to sin against God. It is interesting to note that even for this, the most serious of capital offenses, the death penalty was not always enforced, even in the Old Testament. You will remember that King David took another man's wife and then schemed to have this man, Uriah, one of his best soldiers, put on the front lines of battle. Once Uriah was in this vulnerable spot, David had the troops withdrawn so that Uriah would be killed. Though David was guilty of two capital offenses, God had mercy on him.

We learn from the Talmud that the death penalty was sometimes replaced by lesser penalties. The Talmud is an ancient Hebrew commentary on the law that showed how the law was to be applied and interpreted in certain situations. The provision for capital punishment, by its inclusion in the law, was meant to teach the seriousness with which these crimes were to be treated.

Finally, as we have already mentioned, in the time of Moses there were no permanent prisons. Remember, Moses and the Israelites spent forty years wandering in the wilderness, living in tents. There was no provision for "life in prison without parole." Without the possibility of life imprisonment, there was no way to assure that a murderer, an adulterer, or an idolater living among them would not hurt others or further erode the social order. And so, the death penalty was the only certain way to make sure a criminal would not murder again.

The Case For the Death Penalty

With this brief look at biblical passages as a backdrop, let's take a look at the reasons usually given in support of the death penalty today. There are five reasons most often cited in literature: (1) retribution, (2) deterrence, (3) safety, (4) healing and closure, and (5) economics. The first reason, retribution, is, for many of us, the most compelling personal reason for supporting, or at least being sympathetic toward, the death penalty. When we read of a terrible criminal—a Jeffrey Dahmer, for example—we wonder what would be an appropriate price for this man to pay for heinous crimes in which he has taken so many lives and caused so many people pain. This man seems inhuman to us, and we want him to pay. When I think of someone doing something awful to one of my family members, I find myself favoring retribution and leaning toward support of the death penalty.

The other four reasons pale by comparison, but still they are worth mentioning. Deterrence as a reason for the death penalty relies on the idea that some criminals might be deterred from committing terrible crimes out of fear of being put to death. Some advocates cite concerns for the community's safety in supporting the death penalty. Execution, they point out, is the one sure way of knowing that the criminal will never escape or be released and go on to commit similar crimes again. Some support capital punishment as an opportunity for healing and closure for the families of victims. Still others believe that the state should not have to financially support those who commit heinous crimes for the rest of their lives—an expenditure that adds up to hundreds of thousands of dollars per inmate—when an execution could presumably save the state money. These are the primary reasons given in support of the death penalty as I've heard them articulated through literature on the subject.

The Case Against the Death Penalty

Now let's take a moment to understand the case that is made against the death penalty by those who would abolish it. These persons begin by first noting that though retribution is a strong motivation for putting a criminal to death, what ends up happening is that we engage in a morally questionable act ourselves. The death penalty, in fact, brings society and the state into the act of violence and taking life away. The criminal justice system acts on our behalf. We make the laws and support their enforcement, and thus when someone is given a lethal injection or electrocuted or put to death by hanging or in the gas chamber, we—together as a society—have done this act. We are participants in violence. We tell our children that two wrongs don't make a right, and yet the rationale of the death penalty seems to support that two wrongs will make a right.

Second, those who oppose the death penalty, as well as many who support it, agree that the death penalty has not proved to be an effective deterrent against crime. In fact, "the South accounts for nearly 80 percent of all executions and it's the only region last year [1998] to experience a rise in serious crime" (*ABCNews.com*, December 18, 1999, citing U.S. Department of Justice statistics). This is true, in part, because criminals don't think they will get caught, and if they are caught they don't think they will be convicted, and if convicted they don't think they will be put to death, at least not until after a long appeals process. The only way in which the death penalty could be an effective deterrent would be if it were practiced as it was in the Old Testament, or as it is still done in some countries. Years ago I visited my father while he was living in Saudi Arabia. During my stay, four men were hanged in the public square and their bodies were left on public display for some time. Horrible sights like this *might* serve as a deterrent, but otherwise the death penalty seems to be no more effective as a deterrent than life in prison.

Third, many opponents resist the death penalty because of the possibility that innocent people will be wrongly executed. In 1999 the sentences of nearly 40 percent of death row inmates were either reduced or reversed (U.S. Department of Justice, "Capital Punishment 1999," December 2000). But even with the appeals process, at least twenty-four persons have been executed in the last one hundred years who were later discovered to be innocent, either as a result of another person's confessing to the crime or because of additional evidence uncovered. Have you ever wondered what it would be like to be one of those twenty-four? What if you were wrongly accused of a capital crime, and there were two or three people who, because of mistaken identity, were willing to testify that you were the one who committed the crime? In 1 Kings 21 we see an example of one good man who was wrongly accused by King Ahab and Queen Jezebel and summarily executed.

Fourth, although many murder victims' families have indicated that they experienced closure when the convicted criminal was put to death, many others have said that the death of the murderer could never really bring resolution. Some have actually fought against the imposition of the death penalty, noting that this "solution" only leaves another parent losing a child, or another child losing a parent.

Many note that the death penalty fails to recognize the convict's humanity. Sister Helen Prejean (whom many will know from the book and film, *Dead Man Walking*) notes that all of us are more than merely the person we are at our worst and most awful moment. These who are put to death are human beings with stories and tragedies and parents and sometimes children. This regard for the human being is the message you most often hear from those who work against the death penalty.

I once read a number of stories about death-row inmates as well as those who were put to death. One book I found particularly compelling is *Death at Midnight: The Confession of an Executioner,* by Donald Cabana (Boston: Northeastern University Press, 1996) who was a warden and prison administrator for twenty-five years. Cabana left the prison system and became a vocal opponent of the death penalty after putting to death two prisoners he had come to know personally. He describes in detail both of these executions and his relationship with the people he put to death. One man maintained to his death that he was innocent. In the end Cabana believed him.

The second man, though he was clearly guilty, had been young and confused when he committed the crime. He had grown up in prison during the ten-year appeals process and was a changed person at the time of his execution. If the purpose of punishment is rehabilitation, that purpose had been accomplished. My sense from reading the book was that the author was no "bleeding-heart liberal" writing of these things, but a man who had seen the humanity of his prisoners and was no longer willing to be forced to put them to death. I would commend this book to you.

Two additional reasons are often given for abolishing the death penalty. One is meant to counter the reasons for the penalty, while the other is a practical justice issue. Opponents note that the death penalty is not an inexpensive way to deal with heinous criminals, and that, in fact, it is usually more costly than a sentence of life in prison. This is due, in large part, to the automatic appeals process. Death-penalty cases are automatically appealed to allow for every possible chance to avoid putting to death an innocent person. The appeals process with its legal bills can last years and cost in the hundreds of thousands of dollars, during which the state is also paying money to house and guard the prisoner. At the same time, death-row inmates cannot work in the prison and thus do not offset any of these costs by their labor. The appeals process for those who are not sentenced to death can be much simpler, involving fewer steps, and thus is not as costly.

Finally, it is noted that the death penalty is not applied in an equal and just way. Those who tend to be sentenced to death are disproportionately minorities who have killed whites, and they are largely poor and unable to afford attorneys who might devote more time and attention to their cases.

As you consider these reasons for abolishing the death penalty, any one of these arguments by itself may not be compelling to you as a reason to be against capital punishment, but taken as a whole, they cannot be dismissed.

The New Testament and the Death Penalty (Luke 6:27–36)

And now we need to take another look at the Bible. Earlier we examined the Old Testament texts supporting the death penalty. Now let's turn to the principles and theological perspectives of the New Testament. The New Testament offers us a way of thinking about God and our humanity that is radically different from the "eye-for-an-eye" model found in the Old Testament, a principle that Jesus himself rejected (Matthew 5:38–39). The two Testaments are not contradictory; in fact, the second would not make sense without the first. Yet I believe that the Old Testament is completed by the New Testament and the gospel of Christ.

The central focus of the cross—of Jesus' death and of the entire New Testament—is *mercy for those who deserve death*. It's not just the murderers who deserve death in the sight of a holy God. The New Testament affirms again and again that "all have sinned and fall short of the glory of God" (Romans 3:23).

57

Paul goes on to note, "For the wages of sin is death, but the free gift of God is eternal life in Christ Jesus our Lord" (Romans 6:23). He notes that the "wrath of God is revealed from heaven against all ungodliness" (Romans 1:18) and that "while we still were sinners Christ died for us" (Romans 5:8).

According to the Scriptures we were all sentenced to death under the law. We have, each of us, violated the spirit, intention, and sometimes even the letter of the law embodied by the Ten Commandments. We merit the death penalty prescribed by the Jewish law. But we are a people who have received the mercy of God! We have known that Jesus saved us—that our sin was nailed to the cross! That doesn't mean there are no consequences to sin. Of course there are! But it seems a bit odd for me to promote a death penalty for one person, excluding the possibility for redemption or mercy, while I am only standing before you because of the mercy of God! While I have held to the death penalty based upon my desire for retribution in the face of evil, I am the recipient of a gospel that offers me grace and not retribution!

Not only is mercy the central focus of the gospel, but Jesus himself showed mercy in several contacts with those who were sentenced to death or who merited the death penalty. First there was the woman caught in the act of adultery—you remember her—from John 8. The people were ready to stone her to death, as the law decreed. The law said that she must die, but Jesus, when asked by her accusers what he thought, replied, "Let anyone among you who is without sin be the first to throw a stone at her" (John 8:7). Jesus stopped the execution and showed her mercy.

The second condemned person Jesus encountered was the man dying on the cross next to him; this man was being executed for crimes that merited his death. The "thief on the cross" admitted his guilt. And yet he called on Jesus to "remember me when you come into your kingdom" (Luke 23:42). This man was likely a murderer, and yet, at that moment, Jesus said to him, "Today you will be with me in Paradise." Clearly the main focus of Jesus' ministry, as you remember, was to "seek out and to save the lost" (Luke 19:10). It would be hard to imagine any group of people more lost than those on death row.

Two more New Testament ideas must be brought to bear as you formulate your own position regarding the death penalty. First, I would encourage you to consider how many New Testament figures were sentenced to the death penalty and were legally executed by the state. The first, of course, was John the Baptist, who was beheaded by Herod. The second was our Lord, sentenced to death by crucifixion. The next was Stephen, the deacon, who was stoned to death. Then there was James, the brother of John, sentenced to death for heresy. Only Judas Iscariot and John the apostle were not sentenced to death among the apostles. The rest—Peter, Andrew, Matthew, Jude, James—all ten, according to tradition, were executed. It is puzzling that we Christians who have seen our Lord and nearly all of the early apostles executed under a legal death penalty could be supportive of the death penalty.

Finally, there is the case of the apostle Paul. His story closely mirrors the primary Christian theological assertion that might cause proponents to rethink their position on the death penalty. Here was a man who ordered, blessed, and witnessed the cruel murder of the deacon Stephen (Acts 6:8–7:60; see especially 7:54–60). We read there that a gang of people, in rage, dragged Stephen out of the city yelling at the top of their lungs. Then they began to stone him to death. Meanwhile the witnesses came and laid their clothes at the feet of a young man named Saul (Paul's Hebrew name). Stephen cried out as he looked to heaven, "Lord, do not hold this sin against them" and then he died. And Paul was there giving approval for his death.

Now, if in the justice of God, there ever was a man who deserved an instant and painful death, it was Paul. Justice demanded it. This man inflicted pain on the early church, persecuted the church, and imprisoned the faithful, and in this story he approved and blessed the death of Stephen, one of the most righteous men in the Scriptures. But thank God Paul did not get what he deserved. Instead, you will recall, God brought

Paul to his knees, and to a place where Paul accepted Christ as his Lord and pledged to serve and follow him all of his days. Paul received the mercy of God and knew that Christ's blood was shed for him. Paul deserved death, but Jesus paid the price for him. Look again at the scripture reading from 1 Timothy, where Paul's experience of God's mercy is described:

> **I am grateful to Christ Jesus our Lord, who has strengthened me, because he judged me faithful and appointed me to his service, even though I was formerly a blasphemer, a persecutor, and a man of violence. But I received mercy because I had acted ignorantly in unbelief, and the grace of our Lord overflowed for me with the faith and love that are in Christ Jesus. The saying is sure and worthy of full acceptance, that Christ Jesus came into the world to save sinners—of whom I am the foremost. But for that very reason I received mercy, so that in me, as the foremost, Jesus Christ might display the utmost patience, making me an example to those who would come to believe in him for eternal life. (1 Timothy 1:12–16)**

I recently reread the transcripts of the interview that Larry King conducted with Karla Faye Tucker. Perhaps you remember that in 1998 she was the first woman executed in over one hundred years in the state of Texas. Her case brought together those who traditionally support the death penalty—among them many evangelical Christians, including Pat Robertson and James Dobson—who all pleaded for mercy for her because she had come to Christ while in prison and had experienced what seemed to be a very real conversion. She was not the same woman who had entered the prison years before. And while no one argued for her release, many argued that the death penalty should be commuted to a life term because this person had experienced, in prison, the ultimate goal not only of the justice system but of the gospel: redemption, reformation, and transformation.

The death penalty does not take these things into account. It cannot. Through the death penalty we, the society and state, usurp God's authority, power, and time line, and as Christians we contradict the very gospel we proclaim—that Christ died for us and that the gospel is the power of God unto salvation.

The Forgiveness and Mercy of the Crucified Jesus

Clearly Americans who support the death penalty can make a case for it through selective use of the Scriptures. I feel sympathetic toward their position, especially as I consider the pain inflicted by some criminals upon their victims and families. In addition, it has been my own opinion in the past. At this point you now have to do the hard work of wrestling with these issues, and forging a position that is well reasoned and consistent with your faith.

As we conclude I would remind you that the death penalty is, according to the Scriptures, what each of us deserves. But God, who is rich in mercy, sent a Savior to us, God's son, Jesus Christ, who through taking his place in the gas chamber of his day—the Roman crucifix—paid a debt he did not owe so that you and I could be set free from death. And to that end, I invite you to pray with me that God's justice and mercy may be known throughout our land.

❧　　　❧　　　❧　　　❧　　　❧

Questions for Reflection

1. What Bible passages are the most persuasive for you when you make moral decisions? How are you influenced by (a) Jesus' parables and teachings; (b) stories of Jesus' relationships to people; (c) the laws given in Exodus, Numbers, and Leviticus; (d) the Hebrew prophets; (e) the theological discussions of John and Paul; and (f) the social codes in the Epistles

(the book of James, for example)? If the Bible was written in ancient times and for uncommon situations, if the Bible speaks through various types of literature and the experiences of many people, how can we hear one voice that leads us to know God's will for our lives?

2. Look at the accounts of God's forgiveness of David in 2 Samuel 12:1–15 and God's promises to those who repent in Hosea 14. What do these scriptures tell us about the God of Israel? What similarities do you see in the story of God's mercy to Gomer, Hosea's unfaithful wife (Hosea 3) and Jesus' mercy to the woman accused of adultery (John 8)? Can you name other Old Testament stories that reveal God's mercy as we have come to know it in Jesus Christ?

3. Find out about the work of Sr. Helen Prejean and also about the prison ministry of your denomination (or, if possible, interview someone who does this work). Imagine that you are a prison chaplain. What would you say about God's mercy to prisoners on death row? What scripture passages would you read to them? What would you say to the murder victim's family?

4. Are there groups or individuals in your congregation and in your community that offer ministry to prisoners and to victims of violent crimes and their families? What can groups or individuals do through prayer, letter writing, and visitation? Suggest specific occasions when we can include prayers for prisoners and prayers for victims in our worship.

5. The Amnesty International website reports that although blacks and whites are murdered in roughly equal numbers, in 80 percent of death penalty convictions the victim was white. Why do you think this is the case? Do you think a person's economic status affects the way he or she is treated in our courts? What can we do as Christians to inform our legislators and other government leaders about our views on capital punishment? What are some ways we can bear public witness to God's mercy and justice?

6. Write a prayer of intercession for use by a study group or a meeting of the social justice commission. Include thanksgiving for God's mercy to us in the forgiveness of our sins and ask for courage and guidance as we seek to understand God's will in the matter of capital punishment. Include petitions for wisdom for lawyers, juries, and judges; good judgment for those who govern; the repentance of sinners; God's care for prisoners; and healing for victims and families.

God of compassion, your Son Jesus wept with Mary and Martha at the death of their brother Lazarus: We ask now for your presence with the dying and the grief-stricken. May those who are afraid and in pain see your tears and know your embrace. Give courage to all who are anguished; give wisdom to those who decide the course of another's life. Teach us to show the power of your love that suffers with us in all things and gives us life in abundance. Grant that in life and in death we may sing for joy beneath the shadow of your wing. In the name of the One who died and rose again to reign with you and the Holy Spirit, now and forever; Amen.

CHAPTER FOUR

Euthanasia

So we do not lose heart. Even though our outer nature is wasting away, our inner nature is being renewed day by day. For this slight momentary affliction is preparing us for an eternal weight of glory beyond all measure, because we look not at what can be seen but at what cannot be seen; for what can be seen is temporary, but what cannot be seen is eternal.

For we know that if the earthly tent we live in is destroyed, we have a building from God, a house not made with hands, eternal in the heavens. . . . For while we are still in this tent, we groan under our burden, because we wish not to be unclothed but to be further clothed, so that what is mortal may be swallowed up by life. He who has prepared us for this very thing is God, who has given us the Spirit as a guarantee.

So we are always confident; even though we know that while we are at home in the body we are away from the Lord—for we walk by faith, not by sight. Yes, we do have confidence, and we would rather be away from the body and at home with the Lord. So whether we are at home or away, we make it our aim to please him. (2 Corinthians 4:16–5:9)

❧   ❧   ❧   ❧   ❧

Dr. Jack Kevorkian opened up the subject of euthanasia to public discussion a few years ago with twenty much publicized acts of assisted suicide. A *Frontline* segment, "The Kevorkian File" (PBS, April 5, 1994), asked the question, "Was suicide the only answer for the people Dr. Kevorkian helped to die?" Another question raised by the program was voiced by a medical professional: "These twenty cases are more of an indictment of our medical system than they are of Dr. Kevorkian. Where were these people's doctors?" We might also ask the question: Where were their churches, their pastors, the people from congregations who cared about them?

What Is Euthanasia and Why Talk About It in Church?

A child is born with a medical condition that will take her life in a matter of days. She requires a feeding tube and oxygen to survive that long—without them she will die in hours. A man has discovered that he has a debilitating disease that will result in the gradual loss of all of his physical abilities in the next three years. He will be mentally alert but trapped within a body that no longer works, unable to speak, to walk, to swallow, even to breathe. A woman discovers she has an inoperable brain tumor. She worries that she will be a burden to her husband and children as her condition worsens. Eventually she loses all ability to care for herself and requires her family to clean her, feed her, and carry her. A teenager has lost her battle against heart disease. She slowly slips into a coma. As her heart weakens she is sustained only with the help of a respirator and other life support. Another man has been told by his physician that he has a rare form of cancer that has attached itself to his bones. Not only is there no cure, but the process of dying will be extremely painful.

These are the real life scenarios that happen in cities across our nation every day. You may have been fortunate enough to have avoided being confronted by them personally, but the day will come when you will be touched by a medical situation just as difficult as this. It may be a parent. It could be a friend. God forbid, but it might be a spouse or a child. It could even be you. At such a time you will need to know what you believe about death and about how we die. If you are a Christian, the most important consideration for you will be to know what God's will is concerning how the suffering face death and what is and is not acceptable regarding our treatment of the dying. That is why this chapter is of particular importance and why I hope it will help you reflect on the important questions about death and dying.

It was in situations like those I raised above that Dr. Kevorkian made his name a household word. Dr. Kevorkian offered an option to his clients that was not only controversial but, in fact, illegal in many states. He offered them the option of "euthanasia." Let's take a moment to define the terms as we begin our focus on what may be the most controversial medical issue since abortion.

"Euthanasia" literally means "good death." While this word could be used to describe a host of different concepts, in the common usage today it has come to mean "mercy killing." By this we mean taking another's life, either at this person's request or without this person's consent, in order to alleviate his or her suffering. Dr. Kevorkian has been a pioneer in a form of euthanasia known as "physician-assisted suicide." Physician-assisted suicide takes many forms—from medication pre-scribed by a physician that will allow patients to take their own lives to simple machines like the ones Dr. Kevorkian rigged up to allow his clients to inject themselves with an overdose of a toxic substance, to the direct injection of the toxic substance by the physician when the patient is no longer able to take his or her own life.

The issue of euthanasia is often discussed in conjunction with two additional concepts: "the right to die" and "death with dignity." In this chapter I will examine euthanasia from a pastoral, biblical, and theological perspective, seeking to un-derstand the role our faith plays in the debate as I invite you to formulate your own views of the will of God concerning the issue of euthanasia.

Respirators, Life Support, and Euthanasia

Let's begin with a situation with which many of you have wrestled and which is often associated with, but is in fact quite different from, euthanasia: the issue of life support. Often in the course of medical treatment for grave physical crises it is necessary to use artificial means—respirators, ventilators, heart machines—to keep patients alive. Sometimes when persons are placed on life support the days that follow reveal that the person's condition is irreversible. Often family members agonize over the decision to withdraw life support.

Some have erroneously called this decision "passive euthanasia," perhaps with the hope of winning support for what they call "active euthanasia." Most ethicists, however, do not consider the decision to withdraw life support in individuals who are dying and who can no longer sustain their own life apart from artificial means to be euthanasia. The key distinction is a differentiation between acts of "omission" and those of "commission." When we withdraw medical life support from persons who are dying, it is the disease or physical condition that eventually takes their lives. These individuals would not live without extraordinary medical means. And the use of extraordinary medical means is not generally deemed to be ethically required in terminal situations.

The withdrawal of life support is usually considered morally acceptable under the following conditions:

1. All treatments likely to restore health have been *exhausted*.
2. The patient is already entering the *death process*; he or she will die without life support.
3. Life support is only postponing the *inevitable*; the individual will not recover.

4. The patient does not wish to be kept alive by *artificial means*. This last point demonstrates the importance of having what is called an "advance directive," a signed and notarized document that describes your wishes in the event you are ever incapacitated and on life support.

Allow me to say again that although removing life support may hasten death, it is the physical condition of the patient that results in death. Family members have given permission for the removal of the artificial means that have kept the individual alive, but that act is not the cause of the death.

Understanding Euthanasia

Withholding extraordinary life support from a dying patient, then, is not euthanasia. Neither is a patient's refusal to receive medical care for an illness to be considered euthanasia. Euthanasia is the direct taking of life, either one's own or another's, to alleviate suffering.

The argument in favor of euthanasia is that there is little difference between *allowing* someone to die and *helping* them to die. Those who support euthanasia note that some patients experience long and painful suffering before being allowed to die, and others live in a vegetative state for years before passing on. The burden to the individual, the individual's family, and society is too great, according to this point of view.

The supporters of euthanasia believe that the most humane thing we can do for someone facing terrifying, debilitating, and sometimes painful illness is to help them avoid protracting the pain. They note that we euthanize animals when they are suffering. Why, they ask, would we not use the same mercy in helping humans find deliverance from suffering? Isn't it more humane, they ask, more merciful and loving, to help end another's suffering, rather than prolonging it? And doesn't a prolonged illness in which one must be cared for, diapered, and hooked to machines take away whatever dignity the individual had? Finally, don't we all have a right to die when and how we want? Shouldn't we be allowed, in certain hopeless situations, to take our own lives or invite our friends, family, or doctors to take our lives for us?

Dr. Kevorkian, and millions of others, believe that this is the case. Voters in Oregon twice decided—first by a 51 percent to 49 percent count in 1994 and again by a 60 percent to 40 percent count in 1997—to allow physician-assisted suicide in their state. Other states have had similar legislation in process. Euthanasia has recently been legalized in the Netherlands where physicians had practiced it outside the law for years and were rarely prosecuted. The new law stipulates strict criteria that must be met if the patient is to be euthanized. Society seems to be shifting in this direction. For most of us, the arguments in favor of euthanasia seem quite compelling—it does indeed seem to be a compassionate solution to the serious suffering humans sometimes face.

Before looking at the arguments against euthanasia, let's first be clear about the alternatives to euthanasia. For persons who are facing serious illness, the decision is not simply between living with debilitating pain or intentionally ending one's life. What we have today are a variety of ways to manage and treat pain. Yes, some persons will have diseases that will cause them to progressively worsen, and for many, additional pain will accompany their debilitation. But it is possible to focus on the pain and provide relief for it in one form or another. The American Pain Society, together with the Joint Commission on Accreditation of Heathcare Organizations, recently issued new standards for assessment and management of pain that are already being implemented at accredited medical institutions. The goal is to teach all doctors and nurses to recognize pain and know how to reduce it to the lowest possible level.

And for families who seek help managing the needs of a loved one who is dying, there is the amazing care given by hospice. The people from hospice are teachers, caregivers, and supporters. They help the patient learn how to die and show the family how to make preparations for death. They stand with the family throughout the time of dying.

As I considered Dr. Kevorkian's patients and the way he helped them die—in the back of a van or in a rented cabin, hooked up to suicide machines on which the patient would press a button, releasing a substance that would end his or her life, I couldn't help thinking of the many people I have been with at their death. They died in their homes or in the hospital with their families and friends gathered around them. They too planned their deaths, but in a way very different from Dr. Kevorkian's method. As people have done for generations before, these parishioners fought to live as long as there was a chance of recovery, but when it became apparent that the end of life was drawing near, they entrusted themselves to God's care. They took medication to be more comfortable. When they were ready, they stopped fighting. They began eating less and sleeping more. Often with one last bit of energy they shared affirmations of love and care with their families. Finally they rested their eyes, began to sleep, and gently passed away. I have held hands with family members—sometimes singing hymns, sometimes praying and sharing scriptures—as we stood around the bed of these persons as they died. Often we have experienced a palpable sense of the presence of God and the communion of the saints in the room as the patient died. There is a dignity in this kind of death that is most profound.

A Christian Response to Euthanasia

Now let's discuss a Christian response to euthanasia. First we must remember that we as Christians are called to offer compassion and love to the sick. Jesus said that this would be one of the criteria used at the Last Judgment when he notes in Matthew 25:36 that he will say to the people ready to inherit the Kingdom: "I was sick and you took care of me."

So much of Jesus' own ministry was spent with people who were physically suffering, and his heart led him to deliver them

71

from their suffering, not by expediting their death but by healing them. If you read the Gospels carefully, you will find that Jesus is constantly healing the sick. In Luke 8 we read the story of a woman who had suffered internal bleeding for twelve years. Jesus had compassion on her when she came close to him in a crowd and touched the fringe of his clothes, an act that showed both incredible courage and intense desperation. She was trembling in fear, but Jesus did not condemn her for her efforts to touch him; instead he healed her, called her "daughter," and told her to go in peace.

In these acts of healing Jesus demonstrated both the power of God and the compassion of God. Jesus was showing what we can expect in God's kingdom, and he was revealing his identity by means of these signs. As Christ's followers we are called to carry on the healing ministry of Christ, ministering to those who are suffering, in pain, or facing debilitating illnesses.

The second point that must be emphasized is the need for mercy and understanding. It is one thing to have a moral position that you have carefully considered. But it is an entirely different thing to walk in the shoes of someone who is facing terrible sickness or tragic physical pain, for whom the euthanasia debate is not simply hypothetical. We should be careful about casting judgment. It is hard to know what we would do if we were wearing someone else's shoes.

I recently watched the video interviews of a number of Dr. Kevorkian's clients, taped just hours or days before he assisted them in taking their own lives. Listening to them describe their desire to die, I found it easy to understand how their friends and families could support them in their decisions. So, while I will offer a critique of euthanasia I can also tell you that my pastor's heart goes out to those who have reached other conclusions when faced with their own loved one's suffering.

Having said that, let's look at the biblical and theological teachings as I believe they relate to euthanasia. The first is rooted and grounded in a principle we discussed in the last chapter, namely, that the ending of life is God's domain. In Genesis 9:5–6 we are told that we are not to take another human life intentionally because each of us is created in the image of God, and God alone has this authority. When we intentionally take life, we usurp God's authority and we begin to "play god." Christians believe that God has the power to stop our heart from beating when it is our time. God doesn't need our help in the process. God can see what we cannot see. Sometimes an individual who is near death may linger on for a few days, not for their own needs or purposes but for the sake of another person. How many times I have seen persons live a few days, even a week, beyond what their physicians thought they could, and this extra time played such a key role in preparing the families for their deaths.

In the discussion of euthanasia Christians and Jews both point to Psalm 139:16 where the psalmist declares that, "in your book were written all the days that were formed for me, when none of them as yet existed." God has numbered all our days and knows their duration from beginning to end. The same psalm says that God is with us even if we "make [our] bed in Sheol," the farthest and darkest place imaginable (v. 8). "Your right hand shall hold me fast" says the psalmist (v. 10). Even in the darkness God is there and "the darkness is not dark" when God is with us (v. 12).

Many also note that Christianity teaches that our lives are a gift from God, and that each day is a part of that gift. We are taught by the apostle Paul that even our bodies do not belong to us; they belong to God and are given to us as a gift (1 Corinthians 6:19–20). To choose to end life before God has chosen our end is to reject the gift and possibly the Giver as well.

Finally, Christians believe that God is able to use suffering for our good and for the good of others as well. Suffering is not the enemy of the Christian. Jesus suffered before his death. He knew what it was like to face such things, and he knew what it was to pray for God to take away the suffering. At the same time Jesus put God's purposes before his own desire to end the suffering. Jesus suffered immensely on the cross, but God used that suffering to save the world. Suffering often turns us to

God. Suffering and the Christian's response to it may turn others toward God. Suffering can deepen our faith and it can strengthen our souls. It is a key ingredient to life; it shapes us, brings out the good in us, and makes us what we would not have been otherwise. God is able to bring good out of evil and tragedy. These are the things Christians believe about suffering.

Christianity in the Face of Suffering and Death

This brings us to our final focus: the gospel in the face of suffering and death. As Christians we not only believe but also have experienced the truth that God carries us even through the valley of the shadow of death. We face the most frightening of circumstances with the hope that God will never desert us. We know that suffering is an opportunity to touch others and witness to our faith. There is nothing so powerful as watching persons of deep faith face death; there is a beauty in their facing it and an intentionality that others can only stand in awe of. In part, their confidence in the face of death comes because of what Jesus has done for us.

You see, the power of the gospel isn't simply that God walked among us to show us the way we should live. Jesus wasn't merely a prophet or a great teacher. The central focus of the message of the Gospels is not the sermons, teachings, or even the miracles of Jesus. No, each of the Gospels is focused on the last week of Jesus' life; the week he faced his own cruel death, racked with pain upon the cross. Each paints a picture for us, first of Jesus experiencing our human condition of fear, of grief, of pain, when he cries out in the garden, "If it be your will, let this cup pass from me!" His death on the cross is the focal point: God's Son bleeds; he dies; his family grieves; they suffer the agony of losing a loved one just as we do. But this is not the end of the Gospels. No, the power of the gospel of Jesus Christ comes on the third day, when Jesus rose from the grave! He told his disciples, before his death, "Listen, I am going to die, but I will rise again! I will be back! And one day I will come back for you!"

The power of Easter is never felt quite so fully as by one who is facing death. When the doctors have finished doing all that they can do, the only hope we have—and the hope that sustains us—is that Jesus promised that his followers would spend eternity with him in heaven, and he went on to demonstrate the reality of this promise by his resurrection from the dead. The apostle Paul points to this truth when he writes in 1 Corinthians 15:51–57:

> Listen, I will tell you a mystery! We will not all die [meaning that Jesus could return for us before our deaths], but [on that day] we will all be changed, in a moment, in the twinkling of an eye, at the last trumpet. For the trumpet will sound, and the dead will be raised imperishable, and we will be changed. For this perishable body must put on imperishability, and this mortal body must put on immortality. . . . Then the saying that is written will be fulfilled:
> "Death has been swallowed up in victory."
> "Where, O death, is your victory?
> Where, O death, is your sting?". . .
> But thanks be to God, who gives us the victory through our Lord Jesus Christ.

It is this faith, this certain and sure hope, that allows Paul to write, "So we do not lose heart. Even though our outer nature is wasting away, our inner nature is being renewed day by day. For this slight momentary affliction is preparing us for an eternal weight of glory beyond all measure" (2 Corinthians 4:16–17).

This is how Christians face death and suffering—not by wanting to end it sooner rather than later, though we may have those feelings at times. We face death and suffering knowing that our lives belong to Christ—they are not our own. We face death and suffering believing that in God's good time we will be called home—we don't have to hurry the process. We face death and suffering believing that God is the only rightful authority on when life ends. We face death and suffering hoping that God can use us, and use our suffering, to let God's light shine through us and to bring something good from something evil. We face death and suffering with hope, knowing that the light and momentary afflictions we face are preparing for us an eternal weight of glory.

This concluding point leads me back to where we began. I mentioned that I watched Dr. Kevorkian's taped interviews with persons he assisted in ending their lives. These videos moved me because they brought back a rush of emotions from experiences I have had ministering with people who were dying. Dr. Kevorkian has now helped more than one hundred people to die by taking their own lives. In the last ten years I have also helped more than one hundred people die—not by offering a means of expediting their deaths, but by offering them hope, comfort, encouragement, prayer, and the support of a church family standing with their families and friends.

In the beginning of this chapter I wrote of a number of patients faced with seemingly hopeless situations. The stories were not invented. These were real people that I had the privilege of ministering with before their deaths. The baby who was born with only days to live was one of the babies I have baptized in the neonatal intensive care unit. Her brief life, measured in weeks from the time her mother and father took her home, changed the world for her parents and for all who know them. Last year I buried the man who found out he had a terrible debilitating disease—but not before he and I sat on his back porch enjoying the warm breezes and talking about what heaven would be like. Had he ended his life several years earlier, I don't think he would have come to commit his life to Jesus Christ.

I went to the home of the woman with a brain tumor, and watched as her husband carried her down the stairs, fed her, and cared for her. Far from removing her dignity, the care and love he gave her in her illness was profoundly beautiful. It reflected a kind of dignity I have seldom seen. And even the teenage girl whose family finally removed life support after she slipped into a coma—her life, to the end, had great meaning. As I gathered with her family around the bedside and we prayed for her, there was a sense of great holiness and awe in the face of the mystery of life and death that none in the room will ever forget.

I could go on with story after story of people who faced suffering and death with great dignity and great faith. They were surrounded by people who loved them. They were helped by hospice and physicians to be as comfortable as they could be. They allowed God to use them, even in their dying, to bear witness to God's love, and to teach the rest of us about life. And in the end, they heard God call their names and welcome them to their heavenly home.

A Closing Word About Dr. Kevorkian and "Death with Dignity"

Dr. Kevorkian has brought to the forefront of the American consciousness the idea of choosing the time when you will end your life and doing so as a means of dealing with suffering and pain. But there is another way, a way that includes doctors trained in how to treat pain and hospice workers who support you and help you find comfort, a way in which each day is considered a gift from God and is filled with purpose, a way that recognizes death not as the enemy but as the vehicle by which God prepares us for life, a way in which lessons are learned and taught. This is the way that begins when we have completely committed our lives to Jesus Christ and trust that in his perfect time he will invite us to join him in our eternal home. Dr. Kevorkian calls euthanasia "death with dignity," but I tell you, the real dignity in death comes from those who walk with Christ to the very last day, those who, especially in the face of suffering, let Christ shine through them and then listen for his voice as he calls them home.

This week I had the opportunity to read a short collection of essays written by Dr. William Bartholome, the physician I mentioned earlier, who was also a leader at the Midwest Bioethics Center in Kansas City, Missouri. In 1994 he discovered he had terminal cancer, and over the next five years he wrote a series of meditations describing the experience. These powerful yet short chapters paint a picture of why death is such an important part of life. It is with his words that I close:

> To live in the bright light of death is to live a life in which colors and sounds and smells are all more intense, in which smiles and laughs are irresistibly infectious, in which touches and hugs are warm and tender almost beyond belief. . . .
>
> I had not known this kind of living before. . . . I wish that you could discover what I now know—that this is the only way for us humans to live! ("Living in the Light of Death," [University of Kansas Medical Center] *Bulletin* 45, no. 2 [April 1995]: 52)

❊   ❊   ❊   ❊   ❊

Questions for Reflection

1. What do you know about "advance directives," "living wills," "organ donorship," and "power of attorney"? What are your state's legal requirements for each of these documents? What help can your congregation provide its members in dealing with these issues?

2. What are some of the traditions we associate with Christian funerals? Read one of the "Services of Death and Resurrection" in *The United Methodist Book of Worship* (Nashville: The United Methodist Publishing House, 1992, pp. 139–71; one service is also found in the *The United Methodist Hymnal*, [Nashville: The United Methodist Publishing House, 1989], p. 870). What does this service express about our faith? Read the suggested scripture readings in the service and talk about one of them and why it speaks to your questions and fears. Read and discuss some of the suggested hymns.

3. Read Romans 8:18–24. What do these verses say about suffering? What is the meaning of verses 20–23, which talk about the suffering of the whole creation? What do these verses say about hope? Read Romans 8:37–39. What can congregations or individuals do to minister to those who are suffering?

4. Read Philippians 2:5–11. What does verse 8 mean when it says that Jesus "became obedient to the point of death"? What is meant by having the "same mind...that was in Christ Jesus" (v. 5)?

5. Plan discussion groups on the PBS series *On Our Own Terms: Moyers on Dying*. Copies of the videotapes may be available from a local library or resource center or they can be ordered from *www.pbs.org*.

6. Write a prayer to pray with someone who is facing terminal illness. See the prayers on pages 628–29 of *The United Methodist Book of Worship* for models.

God of all children, your Son showed his disciples how to enter your kingdom by placing a child in their midst. Teach us to come to you as your sons and daughters, listening for the peace of your word in the trouble of the world. Show us the power of silence, the effect of quiet caring, the honor of bearing your name. Teach us to pray ceaselessly and selflessly; guide us to reflect your light. Give us the wisdom and imagination to reorder our lives, to bring your healing touch to those around us, and to lead our children to your embrace. We pray in Jesus' name; Amen.

CHAPTER FIVE

Prayer in Public Schools

Rejoice always, pray without ceasing, give thanks in all circumstances; for this is the will of God in Christ Jesus for you. (1 Thessalonians 5:16–18)

"And whenever you pray, do not be like the hypocrites; for they love to stand and pray in the synagogues and at the street corners, so that they may be seen by others. Truly I tell you, they have received their reward. But whenever you pray, go into your room and shut the door and pray to your Father who is in secret; and your Father who sees in secret will reward you.

"When you are praying, do not heap up empty phrases as the Gentiles do; for they think that they will be heard because of their many words. Do not be like them, for your Father knows what you need before you ask him. (Matthew 6:5–8)

❋   ❋   ❋   ❋   ❋

Over the past few months I have received a similar e-mail message from a number of individuals. Perhaps it has been forwarded to you as well. It begins, "Now I sit me down in school, where praying is against the rule."

I've received four or five similar rhymes by way of the Internet. These e-mails express a growing frustration among many Christians related to the issue of prayer in public schools. And the debate is not merely about prayer in public schools but about the place religion will play in the schools. Over the last two decades a great deal of heat has been generated by what are sometimes called "culture wars" surrounding the issue of religion in the public schools. Unfortunately little light has accompanied all the rancor. My hope today is to bring an informed, biblical, and theological perspective to these issues.

A Brief History Lesson on Religion and the Public Schools

Let's start by going back to the topic that began this series: the separation of church and state. We looked at the First Amendment to our Constitution, which was designed from its inception to protect the basic rights we hold dear as Americans. Look at the First Amendment again:

> Congress shall make no law respecting an establishment of religion, or prohibiting the free exercise thereof; or abridging the freedom of speech, or of the press; or the right of the people peaceably to assemble, and to petition the government for a redress of grievances.

Within this one amendment are three clauses that relate to our theme today. The first is called the Establishment Clause: "Congress shall make no law respecting the establishment of religion." This clause has been interpreted to mean that neither the United States Congress nor any official national, state, or local government body—including schools—shall do anything to give even the appearance of establishing one religion over another. This right was crucial to some churches in the late eighteenth century; it was designed to benefit people like us. It guaranteed that the religion of the majority in a particular state could not become the official religion of the state. Methodists, Quakers, Baptists, and others—at that time we were in the minority—felt this clause was a source of protection from the majority churches, primarily the Church of England, which at the beginning of our country dominated the South, or the Congregational Church, which dominated in New England. Both of these denominations had advocates who wished to make them the official national church.

82

The second clause is called the Free Exercise Clause: "Congress shall make no law...prohibiting the free exercise [of religion]." Again, this protected the basic rights of all religious minorities to practice their faith freely. It made clear that the state would keep its hands out of the religious arena. This is one of the most important guarantees of the Constitution, and it has allowed religion in America to flourish.

The third clause that is often discussed in terms of this debate is called the Free Speech Clause: "Congress shall make no law...abridging the freedom of speech." Once again, we treasure this part of our Constitution allowing each person the freedom to express individual views or opinions even if they are offensive or counter to the opinions of the majority.

These three clauses of the Constitution form the foundation of the debate about prayer in public schools. With these as a backdrop, let's take a look at the historical foundations of our public schools in America.

As you probably know, the first schools founded in America by settlers from Europe were begun by Protestant churches. One of the motivating factors was to teach people how to read the Bible. Reading itself was not necessarily a required skill in the workplace in the eighteenth and early nineteenth centuries, but the Protestants felt that it was necessary for everyone to learn to read the Bible. The Bible, in fact, was used to teach reading and writing for well over one hundred years.

Over time the state began to see the value of an educated populace. American democracy was based on the expectation of informed voters, and eventually more jobs began to require skills learned at school as well. Some politicians,   including President Ulysses S. Grant, began advocating public school education without religious or sectarian influence. Gradually the state and local governments took over the job of running the schools, using tax dollars to fund education. Now the schools belonged to everyone and were paid for not by a particular church but by public funds.

Interestingly enough, the current debate about prayer and religion in public schools is not new. This debate was begun in

83

the mid-1800s between factions within the Christian community. At that time, there had been a recent influx of immigrants from Roman Catholic countries, and the debate was between Roman Catholics and Protestants. Roman Catholics began to resent the daily scripture readings from the Protestant King James Version of the Bible, the Bible instruction that reflected only Protestant interpretations, and the sectarian prayers that were mandatory in the public schools where their children were being educated, which were paid for by their taxes. They felt that what their children were being taught in the schoolroom was often contrary to what they themselves were teaching their children at home, and in some cases teachers were telling children that their parents' beliefs were wrong.

The parents began seeking change by asking that Catholic children be allowed to read from Catholic versions of the Bible. When this request was denied, Roman Catholics initiated efforts to take the teaching of religion out of the public schools. The courts ruled that the Catholics were right, but these efforts resulted in a tremendous anti-Catholic backlash. At one point as many as thirteen Catholics were killed and two Roman Catholic churches burned in response to the attempts to end the Protestant-dominated teaching of religion in the schools. Ultimately the Roman Catholic response was to start the parochial school system where Catholic children could receive an education while being taught Roman Catholic doctrine rather than Protestant doctrine.

By the turn of the century less than half of American schools still included required daily Bible reading and prayer. But for these schools, things were about to change as a result of some landmark Supreme Court decisions that would redefine what is and is not permissible with regard to religion in the public schools. Let's take a brief look at the court cases that would profoundly impact the issue of prayer in public schools.

1962—Engel v Vitale

In 1951 the New York Board of Regents, who oversee the state's schools, wrote a twenty-two-word prayer that it urged local schools to use at the beginning of each day. The exact words were, "Almighty God, we acknowledge our dependence upon Thee, and we beg Thy blessings upon us, our parents, our teachers and our Country." What could possibly be wrong with reciting a prayer like this each day? It did not mention Jesus, and it was accessible for all who believe in God. But Justice Hugo Black, writing for the majority in the *Engel v Vitale* decision, said that the government is to "stay out of the business of writing or sanctioning official prayers and leave that purely religious function to the people themselves and to those the people choose to look to for religious guidance." The argument was that the concept of a school's writing and sponsoring prayer represented the state's sanctioning religious practice and was an opening that could lead in the direction of an established church.

1963—Abington Township School District v Schempp and Murray v Curlett

Almost exactly one year later the Supreme Court decided two additional cases that it heard together, *Abington Township School District v Schempp* and *Murray v Curlett* (a suit brought by the renowned atheist Madalyn Murray O'Hair on behalf of her son). In these cases the justices rejected state laws requiring daily Bible reading and the recitation of the Lord's Prayer in schools, stating that both violated the Establishment Clause of the Constitution.

1980—Stone v Graham

In 1980 the Court ruled in the case of *Stone v Graham* that the Ten Commandments could not be placed in the public schools, even if paid for by private donations, because the Ten Commandments represent particular religious perspectives and the display of them implies state support, not merely of the moral commands, but also of the theological views of a particular religious group. The Court majority noted that the first two commandments forbid the worship of any God but

Israel's God and the fourth commandment requires worship on a particular day. Clearly, they stated, placing the Ten Commandments in the school indicated government support of them, even if the state did not spend the money to post them there and even if the reading of these commandments was not required.

1985—Wallace v Jaffree

In the 1985 ruling, *Wallace v Jaffree*, the Court struck down Alabama's "moment of silence" laws saying that the intention as it is recorded in the Alabama law books is to encourage persons to begin their day with prayer. Once more this represents official encouragement by the state of religion. The Court left open the possibility of having moments of silence in school but rejected any wording that would indicate that these moments were specifically to encourage prayer.

1992—Lee v Weismann

This ruling rejected official school-sponsored prayer at high school graduations. Specifically, the practice of a school's issuing an officially sanctioned invitation to a religious professional from a particular faith tradition to pray at an event that is considered mandatory for public school students was disallowed. The ruling does not restrict the First Amendment rights of free speech for students to say what they choose when asked to give an address at graduation. Students, in other words, can include references to their faith in valedictory speeches or other kinds of graduation remarks, but a prayer cannot be an official school-sponsored and endorsed part of the graduation event.

Proponents of Prayer and Religion in Public Schools

Many have interpreted the Supreme Court decisions just mentioned as a violation of their faith, as a "tyranny of the minority," and as a series of decisions that have led to the decline of our civilization. A Baptist pastor from Mississippi expresses these feelings in response to a case that forced the local school to stop its practice of having morning devotions and prayer broadcast on the loudspeaker each day during class. The town is small, with a population in which Protestant Christians are overwhelmingly in the majority. The students whose parents were in favor of continuing the morning devotions numbered thirteen hundred; the suit to stop the practice was brought by the mother of the one student who opposed them. The pastor in his interview for a news program was visibly upset. "Is it right," he asked, "for one person to tell thirteen hundred kids they can't do it? Is this a democracy?"

There are many who share this view. Those who think the courts are wrong in disallowing school-sponsored prayer go on to make their point by citing the rise in violent crimes, the necessity for metal detectors in schools, the decline of standardized test scores, the rise in teen pregnancies, and a long list of other social problems among young people as a direct result of these Supreme Court decisions. Many folks who hold these views have suggested that starting the day off with prayer might cause students to commit fewer crimes and to think twice before doing harm toward others. Prayer in schools, they suggest, might have hundreds of other benefits, making our nation a safer and better place to live.

In 1994 Newt Gingrich in his "Contract with America" promised to have a constitutional amendment supporting prayer in public schools by 1995. An amendment was drafted but did not have the necessary support to take it through the process for approval. Another key attempt at reintroducing Scripture in public schools came in response to the Columbine High School shootings when the "Ten Commandments Defense Act" was introduced at the federal level, which was aimed at encouraging schools to post the Ten Commandments outside public schools. This measure also died, in part, because of serious concern that it would be struck down by the courts after its approval.

87

In both efforts, and a host of others that have been discussed in Congress since 1962, we find legislators struggling to make laws and to wrestle with issues related to prayer. What is often missing from these efforts is a study of what the Bible actually teaches us about prayer. So, before we move on toward any conclusions, let's look at what the Bible says about this important subject.

The Bible on Prayer

We will examine three scriptures as we consider this issue from a biblical perspective. The first is a command by the apostle Paul that we "pray without ceasing" (1 Thessalonians 5:17). Paul is challenging us to make our entire lives an act of prayer. Our entire lives should be bathed in prayer, from the simple blessing we have as we break the night fast and eat our morning meal, to the drive to work, to the moments throughout the day when we offer the simple prayer of thanks, praise, or request for help. We should be constantly in contact with God. Some people even suggest that the way we live our lives ought to be seen as prayer. We are to pray throughout the day—even at school.

Having said this, we must also note that Jesus taught us to pray in a specific way. Notice what Jesus teaches us about prayer in Matthew 6:5–8:

> "And whenever you pray, do not be like the hypocrites; for they love to stand and pray in the synagogues and at the street corners, so that they may be seen by others. Truly I tell you, they have received their reward. But whenever you pray, go into your room and shut the door and pray to your Father who is in secret; and your Father who sees in secret will reward you.
>
> "When you are praying, do not heap up empty phrases as the Gentiles do; for they think that they will be heard because of their many words. Do not be like

them, for your Father knows what you need before you ask him.

Jesus indicates here that the kind of prayer we offer God as individual Christians is meant to be prayed humbly and without show. Prayer is not a performance and not a sermon; it is not meant to be something we do to impress others but something we do for ourselves. Jesus taught us to pray as individuals when we are alone and recognize our own need for God's care and forgiveness. Jesus' teaching does not preclude group prayers; we offer them in church, and we offer them at mealtime with family and friends. Communal prayers have a wider focus: They are a means of praying on behalf of, for, and with an entire group. They speak for those who share the same faith. But the prayers of our faith community are still given in the spirit that Jesus taught; they are uttered with deep humility and thanksgiving for all that God has done.

Finally, I want to encourage you to study other scripture readings regarding Jesus' own prayer practices. What you will find is that most often when he prays, Jesus withdraws to pray by himself. In Mark's Gospel, for example, we see many examples of this. For instance, Jesus spends forty days in the wilderness alone praying before his baptism (1:9–13). After he chooses his disciples, he goes away alone again to a deserted place to pray (1:35). At one point Jesus notices that the disciples need a place to rest and pray and he says to them, "Come away to a deserted place all by yourselves" (6:31). And on the night before his crucifixion he withdraws again to pray at Gethsemane (14:32–42). It occurs to me that while our nation has been engaged in a loud culture war over prayer in public schools, I am not sure the Christians who are most upset about the rulings against prayer in the classroom have taken the time to consider what Jesus actually taught about prayer!

89

A Bit of Clarification on What Can and Cannot Happen in Public Schools

I encourage you to think and pray about this and to discuss this topic with other Christians. On this issue I speak as a pastor who has devoted my life to teaching people about prayer and leading them to the Savior. It is my deepest desire that people pray. But as I read the Constitution and the Supreme Court decisions, I believe the correct judgments were handed down, both from the perspective of constitutional law and from the perspective of what that law was meant to do. The First Amendment was meant to protect us from having the state force a particular faith upon us, or even favor one religious perspective over another. This has allowed Christianity in the form of multiple denominations and churches to flourish in our country.

The elimination of school-sponsored prayer is an essential part of protecting all of our rights as Christians. My wife and I have worked very hard to shape our children's faith. We make sure they are in church every weekend. We have taught them the Bible, sought to lead them to be disciples of Jesus Christ, and prayed with them constantly. We bring them to Sunday school and youth group to reinforce the faith we have taught them, knowing that the message they hear at church will be parallel to what we've taught them at home. But when I take my children to school, I am taking them to learn about math, science, reading, and social studies.

And while I am counting on the fact that the importance of religion in the arts and history will be included in any study of the humanities, I am also counting on the fact that the school and its teachers will not try to influence my children's choice of faiths or their religious practices. The current interpretation of constitutional law as it relates to prayer in public school is meant to ensure that this will not occur.

Having laid out this position, I would like to clarify what students and teachers can do when it comes to exercising their faith at school. There is available an excellent document first

90

drafted in 1995 and subsequently revised twice. It is entitled "Religion in the Public Schools: A Joint Statement of Current Law." It was drafted by groups representing all sides of the ideological spectrum including the National Association of Evangelicals and the American Civil Liberties Union. According to this document, there are numerous ways we can live out our faith in the public schools, including the following:

Students can
1. pray any time in school.
2. pray anywhere in school.
3. wear clothing with a religious message.
4. share their faith in school.
5. meet for Bible Study after hours.
6. write about religious topics as long as they meet he criteria of the assignment.

Teachers can
1. wear crosses.
2. teach the importance of religion to society as part of social studies classes.
3. study the Bible as literature.
4. discuss the origins of religious days.
5. assign classic literature with religious themes (From "Religion in the Public Schools," provided by the White House to public schools, April 1995).

Our kids need to be praying in school; there's no doubt about it. But they can do this without being directed by the school. They may pray as Jesus guided us to pray—not in order to be seen by others, but quietly, in each person's own way, without forcing others to join them.

Where Will America's Children Meet God?

In my school days, I never experienced prayer or Bible reading as an official part of the school day. I do not know how those of you who went to schools where such activity was

91

practiced were affected. I can tell you that the world today is a very different place than it was in 1955; our culture and our society have changed as the result of a complex set of influences. To claim that the elimination of class devotions brought about the problems we have today is as much of a stretch as to say that posting the Ten Commandments on school walls would have stopped the boys who committed violent murder at Columbine High School.

We have created a culture of violence, one that numbs the minds of children who are often not supported by parents. We've created a culture where drugs, alcohol, and teen sex are endorsed everywhere we turn. We indulge our children with violent toys and video games; we let them see movies or television programs that are saturated with violence. A moment of silence at the beginning of the day would not change these realities. What would change them is a personal and genuine Christian faith. It is through our faith in Jesus Christ and the power of the Holy Spirit working in us that we find the strength, convictions, and power to live as Christ's people.

But it is not the job of the school to bring our children to Christ; it is the responsibility of parents, grandparents, aunts and uncles, friends, and the church. If kids meet Christ today it will be because of churches that are willing to be lighthouses and because, during the hour a week we have these kids in Sunday school, church members take seriously the call to teach and mentor children and lead children to discipleship or because others are willing to be youth group sponsors and youth Bible study leaders. Lives are being changed because of what our Sunday school teachers and youth leaders do. Children's lives are affected by every adult they interact with at church. And more children from our community need to be invited to church. If our children will learn the Lord's Prayer, if they will come to know Noah and Abraham, Esther and Ruth, Joseph and Mary, and most important, Jesus Christ, they will do so because we are doing our job in caring for children and loving them into the kingdom of God!

This brings me to one last word, and that is a word to Christians who are schoolteachers and administrators. Most of the teachers my children have had in school were Christians, and for this I am grateful. Though you cannot overtly seek to bring your students to faith in Christ, you can minister to them. You can encourage children and believe in them. You play such an important role, and God is honored by what you do with your lives. You chose a career that may never pay six figures but that allows you to invest in the lives of our children. Teachers are heroes, and we are all grateful to them. And you as Christian teachers, while you may not intentionally use your position to lead children to the Christian religion, you may certainly let Christ's love shine through you.

You teachers may pray for your children by name in the evenings at home. You may live the gospel in how you love them at school. You may ask the Holy Spirit to work through you as you work with the most challenging of these kids. You may listen for the Lord to guide you in what you do.

In bringing this chapter to a close I would reiterate that prayer in public schools is, in many ways, a nonissue. Our children can pray "without ceasing," at any time, anywhere in their schools. Too often this issue has been used to stir the passions of well-meaning Christians who have not thought through all of the implications of the position they are advocating. We cannot forget, as Christians, that the constitutional separation of church and state as applied to the issue of prayer and devotions in the public schools is an important *protection* for us and for our children. At the same time, it is critical that we as parents are taking responsibility for our children's values; that we are exercising discretion in how we allow them to entertain themselves; that we are leading our children to faith in Christ; and that we are setting an example for them in word and deed regarding what faithful discipleship looks like. These actions—not a mandatory period of silence at the beginning of each school day or the posting of the Ten Commandments on the walls of our classrooms—will help our children take their faith seriously and put it into practice in their daily lives.

Questions for Reflection

1. Read Matthew 6:1–18 and, using Jesus' teachings in these verses, make a list of suggestions for how we should pray. What has to be done for God's kingdom to come on earth (v. 10)? What specific needs are prayed for in the Lord's Prayer? Why do you think Jesus uses only *plural* first-person pronouns in this prayer ("us," "our")? In what way do verses 14–15 relate our prayer life to the way we live and act toward others?

2. Discuss the needs of the children in your church; for example, more Sunday school teachers, mentoring, after school activities, opportunities for them to serve. How can we encourage more children to come to our churches? What are some specific ways that children can learn to be witnesses to their faith without being overbearing or self-serving?

3. The Ten Commandments are good rules to live by, but they are more than that. Walter Brueggemann, in *The New Interpreter's Bible* (Nashville: Abingdon Press, 1994, vol. I, p. 852), says they are the "foundational absolutes of God's purpose in the world....They disclose the non-negotiable will of God." Given this theological understanding, discuss why persons whose religious background comes from other than the Jewish or Christian tradition object to seeing the Ten Commandments displayed on the walls of government buildings. What do the Ten Commandments tell us about God?

4. What is the variation in the meanings of the words "proselytizing," "witnessing," and "evangelizing"? Under what circumstances is each appropriate? How do we balance our call to witness with a need to respect other religious traditions?

5. What casues the violent incidents in which children are the perpetrators? What can congregations or individual Christians do to change the climate of violence in our society?

6. Write a short, simple prayer that a child from your church could learn and pray silently at the beginning of a school day. Write a prayer asking for guidance and courage for the school officials and teachers in your school system; include as many names as possible.

God our maker, from our mothers' arms you have led us on our way and blessed us with countless gifts of love. We thank you for the life your Spirit breathes into us and for your surrounding presence. Search us and probe our thoughts; test us and judge our convictions. Grant us the wisdom to see your design in all that is created; give us the compassion to know the anguish of others. Teach us in all that we do to honor your name. For the sake of your Son, we pray; Amen.

CHAPTER SIX

Abortion

For it was you who formed my inward parts;
  you knit me together in my mother's womb.
I praise you, for I am fearfully and wonderfully made.
   Wonderful are your works;
that I know very well.
  My frame was not hidden from you,
when I was being made in secret,
   intricately woven in the depths of the earth.
Your eyes beheld my unformed substance.
In your book were written all the days that were
formed for me,
    when none of them as yet existed.
                              (Psalm 139:13–16)

One of the Pharisees asked Jesus to eat with him, and he went into the Pharisee's house and took his place at the table. And a woman in the city, who was a sinner, having learned that he was eating in the Pharisee's house, brought an alabaster jar of ointment. She stood behind him at his feet, weeping, and began to bathe his feet with her tears and to dry them with her hair. Then she continued kissing his feet and anointing them with the ointment. Now when the Pharisee who had invited him saw it, he said to himself, "If this man were a prophet, he would have known who and what kind of woman this is who is touching him—that she is a sinner." (Luke 7:36–39)

In this chapter we will deal with what is commonly recognized as the *most* divisive and controversial moral issue of the last several decades: abortion. We come to address this issue as Christians, seeking to bring our biblical and theological resources to bear, and hoping to set aside the heated rhetoric, gross oversimplifications, and raging tempers in trying to clarify our own thinking on this issue.

Unlike some denominations, where a majority of the people could be described as strongly anti-abortion or, in a few instances, strongly pro-choice, my guess would be that individual Christians within The United Methodist Church would more nearly mirror our society as a whole, which seems to be very divided on the issue. Polls indicate that a majority apparently favor keeping abortion legal in the first trimester, but a majority also oppose late-term abortions and abortions performed on minors without parental consent.

As we begin, allow me to mention the special cases I will not address in this chapter: I will not be speaking to the issue of the specific cases of rape, incest, abortion to save the mother's life, or abortion due to fetal abnormality. Each of these requires special attention and arguments for and against that we do not have the time to address in one chapter. Since these reflect a relatively small percentage of all abortions performed, I will leave the discussion of them to another time. Today we will talk about what is sometimes referred to as "elective abortion"—nontherapeutic, nonrequired abortion.

Finally, before we begin, allow me to offer a prediction. I predict that we are nearing the time in which the abortion debates of the past will no longer rage. With the advent of true "morning after" pills, a new generation of contraceptive pills that can be effective at preventing implantation of a fertilized egg even up to three days after conception, the debate will change. In the future, abortion clinics as we have known them will no longer exist. There are still many ethical questions about the use of these pills, but the end result will eventually be a reduction in the number of surgical abortions performed in this country. Be that as it may, today we will focus our attention and thoughts on the relationship of the gospel to the issue of abortion.

What Really Happened in Roe v Wade and Why?

To begin let's go back to January 22, 1973, a day when three major news stories made the headlines: former President Lyndon Johnson died, a peace of sorts was announced in Vietnam, and the Supreme Court would hand down the most controversial decision ever given by the justices—a decision that has divided our nation ever since—*Roe v Wade*.

The late 1960s and early 1970s were times of tremendous change in our country and a time of social revolution. The sexual values of our country were changing. Women were finally making significant headway in gaining critical civil rights. And serious questions were being raised about the right of women to control their own bodies.

It was into this social climate that the Supreme Court agreed to hear a Texas case in which a woman named Norma McCorvey, who had assumed the name Jane Roe to protect her identity, sued the state of Texas for the right to have a legal and safe abortion. Abortions were legal in Texas in order to save the life of the mother, but elective abortions—those not medically required—were against the law.

The Supreme Court heard the initial arguments in the case in 1971, heard the case again in 1972, and gave its ruling on January 22, 1973. Roe's attorneys asked the Supreme Court to find the Texas abortion laws unconstitutional based upon the Ninth and Fourteenth amendments. The Supreme Court ruled in Roe's favor, and with its ruling, dismantled the nation's abortion laws. At the time elective abortion was illegal in forty-six of our fifty states. This ruling brought a revolution.

Many, including at least one of the justices who voted in favor of Roe, have said that the Supreme Court may have overstepped its bounds in the Roe case. Rather than allowing the people and the states to work through the abortion debates, the Supreme Court drafted a decision that would leave little room for compromise, based upon an interpretation of the Fourteenth Amendment that clearly was not understood in this way when it was adopted by the states in the 1860s. The ruling in *Roe v Wade* served to guarantee that the right to an abortion was protected by the Constitution.

In a nutshell, here is the Roe decision: The right to terminate a pregnancy is a matter of personal decision and is a privacy issue protected by the Constitution. Since abortion in the first trimester is deemed to be as safe or safer than carrying a child to term, states cannot restrict abortion rights in the first trimester. Abortion on demand in all fifty states was instantly the result of this first part of the Court's rulings. Later Supreme Court rulings have allowed states to attach certain conditions and requirements to first trimester abortions including waiting periods and parental consent for teenagers. In *Roe* the Court went on to rule that second trimester abortions are more medically challenging than first trimester abortions, and thus the state may regulate these abortions, but only to protect the health of the mother, not for the purpose of restricting abortions per se. Finally, the Court ruled that once an unborn child is viable, that is, when it can survive outside the womb, the state may regulate or even prohibit abortion except when necessary to preserve the life or health of the mother.

In reading the works of some of those who supported abortion rights in the late 1960s or early 1970s it is clear that no one anticipated the results of this decision. What seemed at the time to be the possibility of 400,000 to 500,000 legal abortions a year actually became just over 1,400,000 legal abortions by 1990. The number has declined slightly since then to about 1,200,000 in 1998 (according to the Alan Guttmacher Institute, an organization focused on reproductive health research). Since *Roe v Wade,* thirty-four million abortions have been performed in the United States in twenty-seven years.

For some of you this may be hard to understand, but there truly are thinking, compassionate, and committed Christian

99

people on both sides of this issue. Today there are people all around you in your church who claim Jesus as their Lord but who hold opinions contrary to your own, both those who call themselves pro-life and those who call themselves pro-choice. Let's try to understand how this can be.

Why Some Thinking Christians Support Legalized Abortion

The committed Christians that I know who support legalized abortion do so not because they think abortion is a good thing. Shortly after *Roe v Wade* Dr. William Archer, a "pro-choice" physician who had written on the subject, noted, "No sensitive person feels comfortable about [abortion]. . . . But I believe there are situations in which it is justified, as the lesser of two evils" (David R. Mace, *Abortion: The Agonizing Decision* [Nashville: Abingdon Press, 1972]). Most Christians I know who are pro-choice have said, "I would not personally have an abortion, but I believe there are circumstances in which having an unplanned child is so traumatic for a woman that she should have the right to not have this child."

I am not certain that unless you have ever found yourself in these situations you can really understand what these women face. I have ministered with a number of people who were against abortion, until they were faced with a teenage daughter who was pregnant. I have known of single women who were in their twenties and thirties who recognized that their entire lives would be changed by the shame of having a baby out of wedlock, the struggle of trying to raise a child alone, the mental anguish of considering bearing a child and then giving it up for adoption.

Some of these women had sex forced upon them by boyfriends. Some found themselves alone to face the prospect of having a child when the father ran. Some found that the birth control method they had been using had failed. Some were low-income women who could not feed and care for the children they already had. Some were using drugs themselves at the time of conception and feared the impact of this on their unborn. And though we will not address this issue today, some were raped, some were victims of incest, and some discovered that their unborn children had serious genetic defects.

Those Christians I know who support a woman's right to abortion have done so out of a deep compassion and concern for these women. Often they have known women who became suicidal upon discovering they were pregnant. Some have held these women when they wept over the situations they now faced. Some have known women who, before *Roe*, pursued illegal and dangerous abortions, occasionally resulting in great physical harm or even death, because they were convinced this was their only way out of their desperate circumstances. Some women who face an unwanted pregnancy in the midst of these kinds of crises do not see abortion as "elective," especially when they consider their own mental and physical health and, in some cases, the needs of the children they already have.

Several years ago a man said to me, "I don't have much patience for women who, months into their pregnancy, just up and decide they don't want to be a mommy after all." This man had never walked with a woman who faced an unplanned pregnancy. Had he done so, he could not have made such a calloused and uninformed comment.

Why Some Thinking, Compassionate Christians Oppose Abortion

Having noted why some Christians support legalized abortion, let's turn our attention to the reasons why many Christians strongly oppose elective abortion. I begin by noting that too often those who call themselves "pro-life" have been so passionate about one side of this issue that they have turned many people away from their views. Pro-choice advocates often point to the violence of extremists in the anti-abortion movement and wonder how these people can honestly believe they are standing for the love of Christ while killing abortion

101

providers, acting out with hatred or anger toward those who oppose them, or treating women with unplanned pregnancies with contempt. Others note that some in the pro-life movement, including Roman Catholics, do not allow for any artificial means of birth control and thus limit women's opportunity to determine whether they will have children or not.

But having noted this, it is important to recognize that the vast majority of people who are pro-life are not represented by the extremists. Most people who are anti-abortion are compassionate people. They do care about the concerns of the mother. Some have opened their homes to unwed mothers. Some have started residential programs for teenagers to carry their children to term. Many do feel the weight of the concern for the mother's well-being.

Yet those who oppose abortion do so believing that life is a gift from God. They believe that conception and the development of a child in the womb are miracles and therefore sacred. They believe that only God should take life away. They note that most abortions are not for rape, incest, or genetic malformations.

Abortion opponents look at the amazing development of unborn children in the womb, how by the end of the second month the unborn have all of the characteristics of our own bodies in miniature: toes, fingers, eyes, ears, mouth, and tummy. They point to the unborn at three months when thumbs are being sucked, and movement is happening and say, "How can we simply regard this as so much tissue?"

They note the ability of the unborn to hear and respond to noise, and the beginning of brain activity that occurs as the child continues to develop. They ask the question, "At what point is this growing little one to be considered human?" They point out that the unborn child is called a "baby" when we want a child but a "fetus" when we do not want the child. How can this be, they wonder? It is the same child. Does our desire for the child make it a baby, while our rejection makes it a fetus?

They also note that there is a price to be paid for having an abortion that many are not willing to talk about. They note that many women have emotional scarring from abortion, especially when later they choose to have children. Those in the pro-life movement challenge us to admit that abortion is not simply a choice, nor is it merely terminating a "pregnancy." They long for us to acknowledge that abortion is terminating the life of a developing child, stopping the heartbeat, and destroying a brain that is already active—it constitutes the destruction of a life. It is hard not to be emotional about such a prospect.

Biblical and Theological Perspectives

At the very least my hope has been to open the door to understanding why thinking people can have opposing views regarding abortion. But now we ask, Do the Bible, Christian theology, and the tradition of the church teach us anything with regard to abortion?

We begin by acknowledging that the Bible never specifically mentions abortion. Though it was known and practiced in ancient times, especially in ancient Rome, neither the Old Testament or New Testament address it directly. But there are passages of scriptures that might inform our position on this issue.

The first is rooted in a concept we've discussed in conjunction with three different sermons: the right God claims to determine when life ends. Genesis 9:5–6 makes clear that ending a human life is not within our jurisdiction. This is God's domain. The primary implications of this claim apply to those who are already born, not the unborn. But the principle must inform our views on abortion. Life itself, and the ending of it, is something that God has not given us authority over.

Second, we have this beautiful picture in Psalm 139 and in Jeremiah 1:5 of God shaping each of us in our mother's womb. Until late in this century, God alone peered into the womb to see the child growing. God is said to be at work in the womb, knitting us together. God even knows who we will become and, while each of us is in our mother's womb, God is shaping an individual's character, innate abilities, and physical attributes.

In the story leading up to Mary's astounding "Magnificat" in Luke 1, Mary is pregnant with Jesus, and Elizabeth is pregnant with John the Baptist. When Mary and Elizabeth meet and Mary speaks, John leaps in his mother's womb, a sign Elizabeth takes to mean that the Holy Spirit has prompted even this unborn child at the visit of Mary and the child Jesus in her womb.

In addition, the Gospels paint a beautiful picture of Jesus' love for little children, including a powerful passage in Matthew 18:1–6 where Jesus takes a child upon his lap and says, "Whoever welcomes one such child in my name welcomes me" (v. 5).

Contrary to the popular discussion about choice and the rights we have over our own bodies, the apostle Paul says in 1 Corinthians 6:12–20 that Christians have a different perspective on an individual's dominion over his or her body. Our bodies are not our own—they are gifts from God—and God still claims ownership of them because we were "bought with a price." In fact, Paul says our bodies are "members of Christ" and "[temples] of the Holy Spirit." For these reasons we are to "glorify God" in our bodies.

Finally, among biblical passages, we would have to look at Mary's story as indicative of how God works. God took a thirteen-year-old unmarried peasant girl and placed within her womb a child who would save the world. This reminds us that God takes the unlikely, difficult, and painful circumstances we find ourselves in and uses them to do God's work.

Moving beyond the Scriptures, it is important to note that while the Bible doesn't specifically mention the word *abortion*, the early church did discuss it, and it was universally condemned. Clement of Alexandria, for example, who lived about 200 CE, said that abortion destroyed what God had created and was an offense against the command to love our neighbor. In the sixteenth century a Jesuit, Thomas Sanchez, argued that an abortion to save the life of a mother was "more probably" lawful as long as the fetus was not "ensouled" (Daniel Callahan, *Abortion: Law, Choice and Morality* [New York: Macmillan, 1970], 410–12). Before 1960 there were no Christian churches in the United States that I am aware of that did not speak against abortion.

The United Methodist Church has taken a strong position on abortion that is often misunderstood. I would like you to read this, from our *United Methodist Book of Resolutions:*

> The beginning of life and the ending of life are the God-given boundaries of human existence....In continuity with past Christian teaching, we recognize tragic conflicts of life with life that may justify abortion, and in such cases we support the legal option of abortion under proper medical procedures. We cannot affirm abortion as an acceptable means of birth control, and we unconditionally reject it as a means of gender selection. (p. 44)

While allowing for the possibility of abortion under certain "tragic" circumstances, the position rejects abortion as a means of birth control, which is the primary reason for most abortions that are performed today.

Stories of Women Who Have Faced a Decision Concerning Abortion

All that we have said so far may seem clinical and hypothetical. So I want to tell you about various members of our congregation, mostly women, who have sent me their abortion stories or perspectives on abortion. A number of the e-mails were from women longing to adopt children, who have tried to have a child but could not. One was from a woman whose adopted child I recently baptized. She noted that the child's birth mother had considered an abortion, but now, seeing her child with these parents, she was grateful that she had not made that choice. This child is now a part of our church family.

105

One of these e-mails has influenced my thinking on abortion more than any other. The woman writes that she was seventeen and her boyfriend was sixteen when she conceived. He had invited her to a party at the home of a boy whose parents were out of town. It was something of a couples' party and most of the kids there were juniors and seniors in high school. After a time the kids paired off and went to the bedrooms. It was that night that this woman became pregnant.

She tells how, when her father found out about the pregnancy, he was furious. These were the days before *Roe v Wade* and legal elective abortions were not available. So her father set up an appointment with a doctor in Switzerland and was preparing to fly her there for the procedure. But she refused to go. She and the boy were determined to marry and have the baby. She writes, "My father told me I would never be welcome in his home again if I went through with the marriage and delivery of the baby."

She moved in with the boy's family and they quickly married. They moved to Arizona to give birth, as having a child so soon after being married would have caused a great deal of embarrassment. The young couple struggled over the next few years, barely making ends meet. Neither one had a high school diploma, and there was no chance for college. After twelve years their marriage ended in divorce. This woman's future was radically changed by her pregnancy and her choice not to have an abortion. Her childhood was cut short. She never graduated from high school and she did not go to college. She was a single mother. I wondered if she regretted her decision. But she went on to write:

> Yes, my life changed dramatically due to the pregnancy prior to marriage, but to this day, that child has been the greatest blessing to me and thousands of others....God has blessed me more with this son than I can ever imagine being blessed. I am so proud of the husband and father that he has become. So many times when I look at him, I think that this incredibly kind-spirited person could have ended up aborted, but instead, due to the classes in Sunday school week after week

that taught me as a child, I knew that even from the moment he was conceived, he was a gift from God. I look back sometimes at the college that I missed, the experiences that "could have been," and thank God that I chose God's way. My life is different than it could have been, but I wouldn't change it for anything.

Thank you, Adam, for being my "gift from God." There can be no greater gift than that of a child that God wants to be born. I never dreamed thirty-six years ago while I was carrying you that you would have the impact on God's people—and me—that you do. You are my pastor, my confidant, and my best friend.

I love you,
Mom

This is *my* story, and this letter was written by my mother. And what it reminds me of is a powerful gospel truth: God takes what we think of as "mistakes," "accidents," and "blunders," and redeems them. This is God's specialty. God knits us together in our mothers' wombs and has plans for each child. God can work—sometimes through birth parents, sometimes through wonderful adoptive parents who could never have a child of their own. But those children have potential. They grow up. I am one of those children.

God's Grace Is Sufficient

I want to end by speaking to you who regret having had elective abortions. I received e-mail from other women who described the difficult circumstances they found themselves in and the choices they made. One woman wrote of her experience, years ago, as she went for an abortion. She described what other women have written about: the emotional scars they carry from the experience. She writes, "The worst part was the total emptiness I felt when I got back to my car. I cried; I cried hard, painful, aching, body-wrenching tears. I would do this for the next six months until the pain, the grief, and the guilt got to be so much that I finally overdosed. Nobody tells the girls this part. Nobody tells them the fact that no matter how long it has been, you will always remember and wonder and long for that child."

God longs to embrace you and wipe away your tears. It is right that you cry before God and ask for God's help. But know this: God is longing to forgive you, to make you whole again. God knows the anguish you feel. The little ones, even those who have been aborted, belong to God, and God will continue to take care of them. We cannot know everything that God has planned for their lives. But we can say that they belong to God. We also know this: God understands the pain, the difficulty, the burden you may feel. If you carry feelings of guilt from an abortion in your past, God is saying to you today, "I understand your heart. I know what happened. I am ready to forgive. This is why I sent my Son—to deliver you. I love you."

This brings me to one last story—the story of Jesus, sitting at table at the home of Simon the Pharisee, when a woman of the city who was a sinner comes to the home. She brings to Jesus an alabaster jar with perfume. She lies at his feet weeping and wiping his feet with her hair. Why is she weeping? Could she be weeping for the mistakes she has made, the times she has turned her back on what she knew was right? Maybe she is weeping because this is the first man who truly made her feel loved. Or perhaps because she so wants to feel his love, his grace, to feel new and clean and whole. And Jesus offers her exactly this. He accepts her tears, he accepts her touch, and he forgives her and loves her.

This same Jesus is present for all of you, for you who have done things you wish you hadn't done; for you who have turned your back on him in the past; for you who felt trapped and couldn't see any other way. For you he came. For you he died. And for you he waits to offer you his grace, mercy, love, and peace.

Questions for Reflection

1. Read 1 Corinthians 6:12–20. What specific concerns about daily activities—what we eat and drink, how we treat others, prevention of illness, unhealthy practices and attitudes, for example—are affected by Paul's view of the body? What does it mean to be "members of Christ" (v. 15)?

2. What part does our community of faith play when we make ethical decisions? What is our basis for decision making when an individual's needs seem to be in conflict with the needs of the community? What support does the community offer to those who make a choice that puts communal good above their own wishes?

3. In the Jewish and Christian tradition, children are considered a blessing and the responsibility of the whole community. Discuss specific ways our denomination, as well as individuals and congregations, can contribute to the welfare of the children among us. How can we include children in the life of the congregation? What duties do nonparents have to the children of fellow church members to nurture their faith, to help them discern their vocations? Do you think we have any special obligations to women who have decided on principles of faith not to have abortions and are raising their children under difficult circumstances?

4. What can we do as a congregation to teach teenagers an alternative to the self-indulgent sexual ethic portrayed in many television shows, movies, and music videos? Listen to teenagers in your congregation to find out more about the struggles and challenges they face in their social life, especially in regard to sexual and reproductive practices. What problems do they see that are new to this generation?

5. Children sometimes suffer as a result of political disputes (see Matthew 2:16–18, for example). What examples in history or in our own time can you name of children being used as political pawns? What responsibility do we have for children in countries that are suffering from violence or political sanc-

tions? What policies could we support that would work to alleviate overpopulation and high infant mortality rates in poor nations?

6. Write a prayer that includes petitions for mothers; for children; for fathers; for women and men who want to be parents and cannot; for the health and safety of all pregnant women; for nurturing adults who care for children; for doctors, nurses, and counselors; for guidance for our community; for forgiveness and tolerance.

Merciful God, we come to you aware that we see now as in a mirror, dimly, that we know only in part. Open our minds to know your grace; call us to meditate on your teaching day and night; order our steps to follow your word. We ask for the light of your presence that we may see others through Jesus' eyes. Give us compassionate hearts and discerning minds that we may embrace others in your name and know what is truly acceptable in your sight. Grant that your church may be faithful and live in peace. We pray in the name of Jesus, who loves us and gave himself for us and all the world; Amen.

CHAPTER SEVEN

Homosexuality

For this reason God gave them up to degrading passions. Their women exchanged natural intercourse for unnatural, and in the same way also the men, giving up natural intercourse with women, were consumed with passion for one another. Men committed shameless acts with men and received in their own persons the due penalty for their error.

And since they did not see fit to acknowledge God, God gave them up to a debased mind and to things that should not be done. They were filled with every kind of wickedness, evil, covetousness, malice. Full of envy, murder, strife, deceit, craftiness, they are gossips, slanderers, God-haters, insolent, haughty, boastful, inventors of evil, rebellious toward parents, foolish, faithless, heartless, ruthless. They know God's decree, that those who practice such things deserve to die—yet they not only do them but even applaud others who practice them.

Therefore you have no excuse, whoever you are, when you judge others; for in passing judgment on another you condemn yourself, because you, the judge, are doing the very same things. You say, "We know that God's judgment on those who do such things is in accordance with truth." Do you imagine, whoever you are, that when you judge those who do such things and yet do them yourself, you will escape the judgment of

God? Or do you despise the riches of his kindness and forbearance and patience? Do you not realize that God's kindness is meant to lead you to repentance? (Romans 1:26–2:4)

❈   ❈   ❈   ❈   ❈

With this chapter we come to the conclusion of our look at Christianity and the controversial issues of our time. We have saved the most challenging issue for last. Some have predicted that The United Methodist Church will divide in the next fifteen years in response to this debate. And my denomination is not alone; every mainline church in the United States is struggling with this issue. Presbyterians, Episcopalians, Lutherans, Disciples of Christ, Roman Catholics—all are wrestling with an issue that will not go away.

I would like to begin by clarifying the position of the denomination to which I belong on the issue of homosexuality. From there we will examine both sides of the debate. Finally, we will try to discern God's word to us today.

The United Methodist Position on Homosexuality

The Book of Discipline of The United Methodist Church represents the binding rules and laws of our denomination. I, as a pastor, am bound by these laws, and members of a United Methodist congregation must function according to them. Our *Discipline* has the following laws that are binding and that represent the official position of the Church. Here's the stance in a nutshell:

1. *No homosexual unions shall be performed in our churches.*
   "Ceremonies that celebrate homosexual unions shall not be conducted by our ministers and shall not be conducted in our churches" (¶ 65C).

113

2. *No church funds shall be given to organizations that promote the acceptance of homosexuality.*
   "The council shall be responsible for ensuring that no board, agency, committee, commission, or council shall give United Methodist funds [apportionments] to any gay caucus or group, or otherwise use such funds to promote the acceptance of homosexuality" (¶ 806.12).
3. *Self-avowed, practicing homosexuals may not be ordained.*
   "Since the practice of homosexuality is incompatible with Christian teaching, self-avowed, practicing homosexuals are not to be accepted as candidates, ordained as ministers, or appointed to serve in The United Methodist Church" (¶ 304.3).
4. *United Methodists are committed to supporting civil liberties and human rights for homosexuals.*
   "Certain basic human rights and civil liberties are due all persons. We are committed to supporting those rights and liberties for homosexual persons....Moreover, we support efforts to stop violence and other forms of coercion against gays and lesbians" (¶ 66H).
5. *All persons, including homosexuals, are individuals of "sacred worth." We are committed to ministry for and with all persons.*
   "Homosexual persons no less than heterosexual persons are individuals of sacred worth....Although we do not condone the practice of homosexuality and consider this practice incompatible with Christian teaching, we affirm that God's grace is available to all. We commit ourselves to be in ministry for and with all persons" (¶ 65G).(*The Book of Discipline* [Nashville: The United Methodist Publishing House], 2000).

It is this last statement that captures the essence of the tension within mainline Christianity regarding homosexuality—the tension you will sense throughout this essay—between the love and grace of God and the biblical witness regarding homosexual practice.

Why Do Some Wish to Change Our Denomination's Stance on Homosexuality?

During the last two years The United Methodist Church has most often been in the news as it relates to three separate incidences of United Methodist pastors' performing homosexual unions in direct violation of the *Book of Discipline*. One story, that of the Reverend Gregory Dell of Broadway United Methodist Church in Chicago, who was suspended after he performed a homosexual union, was captured in an interview on the Los Angeles UPN television affiliate. In this interview Dell defended his position by saying that he felt his actions were "consistent with the direction of our denomination and our faith, a faith and a denomination that have historically embraced people in all their differences and individuality." More recently, a group of sixty-seven United Methodist pastors from the California-Nevada Annual Conference together presided at a ceremony celebrating the union of a lesbian couple.

Some of you would ask, "How can these pastors possibly support homosexual marriages, the ordination of homosexuals, and the acceptance of homosexual behavior?" Let's consider the answer to that question for a moment.

Those who support changing the church's position regarding homosexuality, opening the door to homosexual unions, and the ordination of homosexuals, *do so out of a keen sense of God's love for all people.* They are thoughtful, committed Christians, not, for the most part, what some would call "flaming liberals." They maintain that they value the family and the traditional covenant of marriage. But as they have come to know homosexual people, as they have listened to their stories, prayed with families, and wrestled with these questions, their hearts have been filled with compassion. They want to

115

extend the love of Jesus to all people. They feel called to embrace the outcasts of our day as Jesus embraced those of his day. There are a number of reasons why they have been so moved by this issue, among which are the following:

1. Homosexuality is not a choice. These pastors and laypeople believe that for many (perhaps most) homosexuals, their orientation was not chosen *by* them, but rather, it was chosen *for* them. They believe that some homosexual persons seem to be wired this way from the womb. Physiologists and geneticists studying the origins of homosexual orientation are finding evidence to support several possible causes. Though their research is not yet conclusive, a number of scientists find indications that sexual orientation may be tied to a human gene. Others see differences in human chemistry or brain structure as leading inevitably to a particular sexual orientation. In addition, many who view homosexual orientation as inescapable for certain people acknowledge that some homosexuality may also be shaped by early childhood experiences, either from the environment in which the children were raised or as the result of an early traumatic experience, including the fact that some homosexuals report being sexually abused as small children by older males or females.

2. Homosexuality in teenagers often leads to despair. Some advocates who want to change our Church's position on homosexuality point to the tragedy of the high suicide rates among teenage homosexuals and note the despair many teenagers feel upon discovering that they are different. These feelings are often exacerbated in the one place where they should be able to find acceptance and love: the church. They feel rejected not only by their families and friends but also by God. The argument here is that if our Church were more open to homosexuals, we would be better able to help young people who are homosexuals understand that God loves them just as they are. These teenagers and their hurting families need to find a safe place in the church where they can grow in faith and feel the love of a community.

3. *Jesus wouldn't reject homosexuals, but would welcome them.* Some note that too often churches have implicitly and sometimes explicitly pushed homosexuals away from God while *Jesus* was always in the business of drawing people *to* God. *They note that Jesus never once said anything about homosexuality,* even though it was practiced in his day, and no doubt there were persons who struggled with homosexuality in the crowds that he ministered to. In contrast to Jesus' compassionate approach, there are pastors across the country who make it their business to preach about, and against, homosexuality on a regular basis. And this preaching itself has pushed homosexuals out of the Church.

4. *What about the homosexuals who have the gifts, calling, and faith to be pastors?* Some of our pastors and laity note that there are many persons who exhibit a profound sense of calling, have all the gifts for ministry that a church could ever want—gifts of preaching, compassion, justice, administration, and people skills—and who are deeply committed to Christ, but who wrestle with homosexuality. Surely God intends them to use these gifts for ministry.

5. *The biblical texts that refer to homosexuality have not always been interpreted with sensitivity and in light of new cultural and scientific understandings.* What of the biblical passages prohibiting homosexual practice? How do these Christians who support full acceptance of homosexuals and homosexual practice deal with the Bible? One typical answer is that the biblical texts prohibiting homosexual behavior refer to certain types of homosexual behavior that are generally condemned as reprehensible—most often slavery, prostitution, and pederasty—and not to monogamous homosexual practice. They also note that in biblical times the concept of "orientation" was not understood: People then could not know that some persons are born predisposed to homosexual feelings and drives. Finally, some simply point to the fact that this is a different time period from biblical times, and the prohibitions against homosexuality—like those against women speaking in

117

the church—are tied to the cultural and historical setting and do not represent the timeless word of God on the issue.

For those who hold these positions, it is very hard to see how a thinking, compassionate Christian could feel otherwise. Because they believe this issue to be so important and because they believe it strikes at the heart of the gospel of Jesus in reaching out to all and sharing the love of God, the proponents of this view feel compelled to work toward and for a change in the denomination's position. Sometimes they are even willing to disobey church law if that is what it takes to be heard and to bring this issue to the forefront of the denomination's consciousness.

Why Is Homosexual Practice Said to Be Incompatible with Christian Teaching?

On the other side of this great debate are people who believe that the practice of homosexuality is "incompatible with Christian teaching." The majority of clergy and laity within our churches do believe that homosexual practice, like many other ways people exercise their sexuality, is not God's will for us. At the same time most in my denomination believe the Church should be in ministry with persons who are of homosexual orientation. Unlike the clergy in some denominations, every United Methodist pastor I know would not only welcome gays into their churches, they would love them.

Yet while ministering to and loving the homosexual person, many pastors believe that practicing homosexual intimate relations is not God's will for our lives. Let's talk about the reasons why they believe this.

1. The witness of the Bible is explicit. First, the Bible explicitly teaches that homosexual sex is not God's intention for us. This side in the debate believes that, even taking into account the arguments of those who seek to narrow the focus of the biblical injunctions against homosexual practice, the clear teaching of both the Old Testament and New Testament is that homosexual intimacy is not God's plan for what we do with our bodies, just as some acts of heterosexual intimacy are also not part of God's plan.

Those who hold this view point to Leviticus 18:22 where we read that a man should not lie with another man. This is found in the context of an entire chapter on sexual relations that are prohibited by God. A second parallel reference is found in Leviticus 20:13. Some point out that these laws are included in the "holiness code" of Leviticus, which includes other prohibitions that we do not hold binding today. And this is true. But their immediate context is a section dealing with sexual practices God does not wish for us to participate in, prohibitions that most would agree are an expression of right and wrong we all would affirm today. Even so, those on this side might give more credence to the less restrictive interpretation if the prohibition against homosexual acts were not repeated in the New Testament.

The New Testament specifically mentions words usually associated with homosexuality three times, and hints at it in a fourth passage (Jude 5–7). In 1 Timothy 1:10 there is a list of categories of "sinners," which includes the Greek word, *arsenokoitai,* which was usually translated as "homosexual." All of the practices in this list are said to be contrary to sound teaching and what conforms to the gospel. In 1 Corinthians 6:9–11 Paul offers another list of those who are living lives contrary to God's plans including male prostitutes and homosexual offenders. Some note that these two types of "offenders" could be linked together to refer to a specific vice called pederasty (a practice in which an adult male dominates a submissive minor male for sexual purposes). Others note that by condemning pederasty, the passage would be condemning what may have been the dominant and most culturally acceptable form of homosexual practice in Paul's day, though it is not acceptable today. Finally, in Romans 1, in the verses quoted at the beginning of this chapter, we read a straightforward passage in which Paul includes homosexual practice as an expression of our sinful nature.

The weight of these passages becomes even more significant, according to those who believe homosexual practice is not God's will, when we consider that the culture in which the New Testament was written generally accepted homosexual practice. If this is the case then the New Testament authors were not simply recording what was the cultural norm and calling this God's will—they were actually confronting what was a culturally accepted practice. While some have suggested that scriptures related to homosexuality are culturally bound like scriptures related to women's rights or slavery, and may be disregarded, it is, in fact, exactly the opposite. In the case of slavery, this practice was a dominant cultural, political, and economic factor of life in biblical times, and the biblical authors could not conceive of a world without slavery, hence they merely gave guidelines for how slaves should live and how masters should treat their slaves. They were blinded by their culture. Likewise, in the case of women's rights, the culture said that women were property, but Paul said they were to be loved as Christ loved the church. Nevertheless, Paul cautioned the churches not to arouse the suspicions of their neighbors by encouraging women to engage in what would be considered outrageous behavior for the time by teaching or speaking in the church. Again, in this case, Paul was influenced by his culture, rather than confronting the cultural norms.

But when it comes to homosexuality, Paul adopts a thoroughly critical stance toward the surrounding culture. Homosexuality was commonly practiced in the Roman world. It was an acceptable part of the culture of the day, and yet Paul includes it as something that, despite approval from the culture, was not God's will.

2. Why God says some things are wrong. In addition, those who believe that homosexual relationships are clearly forbidden by the Scriptures note that homosexual relationships often bring harm to the persons involved, both emotionally and physically. This viewpoint maintains that God prohibits certain things *because God loves us and does not want us to be hurt.* They note that God designed our bodies for heterosexual relationships—again pointing to God's will found in our design—and that when we use our bodies in ways that are contrary to the purposes for which they were designed, we can hurt ourselves.

3. *God's help makes anything possible.* These Christians within our denomination want homosexuals to know that they are loved and that they can live a life in accordance with the Scriptures. They are not necessarily advocating that homosexuals change—they acknowledge that such change is unlikely—but they believe that persons can, with the help of God, lead celibate lives.

Persons who hold this position maintain that some homosexuals are able—with the help of counselors, friends, and the Holy Spirit—to see their desires reshaped and sexual energy redirected toward intimate male-female relationships. No one believes this transformation is easy, but these advocates say that it is possible and point to testimonies of those who have made this change with God's help. In addition, they point to the fact that many people, for spiritual as well as other reasons, choose lifelong celibacy and that this choice is affirmed as among the highest callings by Jesus and by the apostle Paul (Matthew 19:10–12; 1 Corinthians 7:8–9, 32–35). Finally, they point to the fact that both Jesus and Paul indicated that God's power is strong enough to help us either to overcome our struggles or to live with them in a way that honors God.

4. *All are born broken; we all struggle with our human condition.* Finally, those pastors who believe homosexuality is not God's will for us often recognize that some people are born with a predisposition toward homosexuality, but they believe that this by itself *does not indicate that God has made one to be, or wishes one to be, homosexual.* We are all born with an orientation to sin. We have a broken and fallen human nature, which means that by nature and from birth, we struggle with our longing for power and wealth, our tendency to be self-centered and self-absorbed, and with a host of issues related to misuse of our sexuality, not simply homosexuality. We may indeed have heterosexual longings and needs that are

not part of God's intentions for the way we live. These are deep-seated issues about which we often feel powerless to change. We are born with a "bent to sinning," as the hymn says, but God encourages us to allow the Spirit to work in us to rise above these things.

Biblical Principles and the Community of Love

I have tried to articulate, as best as I can in a very brief amount of time, the arguments on either side of this debate. Before sharing my own views on this issue, there are several things we must agree upon, and several questions I would encourage you to wrestle with, regardless of how you come down on this issue.

Two scriptural principles are key for us to live and practice: The first is that we are to "bear one another's burdens" to help one another with our struggles, and to encourage one another in Christ. The second is that we are to "love [our] neighbor as we love ourselves." We must be willing to respond to one another in this way, and this includes the Church's response to homosexuals.

In addition we must see others through the eyes of Jesus. Jesus' only words of condemnation were uttered against self-righteous, religious people, not against those who wrestled with lifestyles that were not biblical, or were unhealthy. He looked with compassion upon people. He taught, nurtured, and loved them. If he did that for us, how much more can and should we do that for others?

There are many homosexual persons in our congregation who, for the first time in their lives, have found a Christian community where they feel wanted and loved, where homosexuality is not the subject of judgmental and self-righteous sermons, and where they can seek to grow in Christ. The challenge to churches is to nurture such a community where all people—gays and lesbians included—can find that Jesus does love them, that God does want them, and that all are valued in God's sight.

When we struggle, when we feel alone, when we are seeking to find meaning in our lives and to know right from wrong, when we need a community who will surround us with love, when we are facing death or pain, the one place for us to go to find the way, the truth, and the life is Jesus Christ. The gospel of Jesus is good news, news that is relevant for our daily lives. That is what I've sought to demonstrate in this book—that being a Christian is where we find answers and peace and hope.

Where I Stand

Now, on to my position as a pastor. I must tell you this is very hard for me. I know that there are at least one hundred, and perhaps as many as two hundred, homosexual persons in my own congregation. At least a half dozen are persons who have shared with me their stories. They worship in the midst of us every week, seeking to grow in their walk with Christ. They participate in missions activities and are involved in Bible study; they invite their friends to church and share the love of Jesus with others. They pray, they seek the Lord, and they are experiencing the transforming power of the Holy Spirit in their lives. This is, for many, the first time in their adult lives they have come back to Christ. I love these people; they are the Lord's sheep, and I am their earthly shepherd.

I say to those who come to my church that if you are gay, I want you to know that I want to be your pastor, that I would be honored to be your pastor, and that you are welcome in our congregation. We want church to be a safe place for you to come, where you will be seen for the person you are. I would go to the wall for the gay and lesbian members of my congregation. The church will love you and I will love you.

That is what my heart wants to say, and it is what I genuinely feel. And it is where I would like to stop. I would like to stop here because I do not want to be lumped together with the fundamentalists who oppose homosexuals and hurt them, because my pastor's heart wants to love people and draw them to Jesus and not push them away, because I keep seeing in my mind's eye several of our homosexual members who are growing in Christ and I don't want to crush their spirits.

But I have also bound myself to the Scriptures; I seek to live according to the Bible's teachings, though I fail in so many ways. It remains the clearest picture I have of how God would have me live my life. So I must consider not only my heart, but also what the Scriptures say on this subject. Once I have done my best to understand the Scriptures, to consider them in the light of their historical context and culture, and to discern where God was speaking a timeless word to us, then I am bound to try following them. As I have studied the Scriptures and read the latest books by those on both sides of the debate, I find I agree with much that those wishing to embrace a change in our denomination's stance have said. But when it comes to the biblical and theological issues, I find that I cannot dismiss the New Testament witness so easily. My study of the Scriptures leaves me persuaded that homosexual practice is not God's highest and best will for our lives.

There are many things that I am naturally wired for, but which I cannot pursue, because I believe that God has something better for me. I have a natural predisposition to do things that will hurt me, or hurt others, or that will dishonor God. Some of these desires and longings are easy to resist, but some require, at times, all of the strength I have not to act upon them. I ask for God's help, and when I fail, I ask for God's grace. In reading the Scriptures, homosexual practice is included in a category of sins that are common to most of us. I cannot dismiss these passages and say they don't matter. What I can say is that as we seek to grow in Christ, the Lord will give us the strength to follow the Scriptures, and the grace when we fall short. If, on this issue, God's will is that homosexual practice be embraced, then we will know, by the continuing disclosure of

God's gracious will to redeem humanity, that God has called for a change. But I cannot say this on God's behalf.

I will admit that even saying these words leaves my heart heavy. I believe they are true and faithful to the Scriptures. But I feel the weight of knowing the struggles homosexual persons have had—with their families, their friends, their churches, within themselves, and with God. I want to cry out to God and say, "Why don't you do something to help them?" And yet, I know that God has. God came and walked among us in Jesus to show us his love. Jesus was constantly reaching out to broken people—not condemning them, but caring for them, forgiving them, and loving them. Ultimately he died on a cross to redeem them, and us, from sin.

This brings me to our scripture passage in Romans 1 once again. At first glance this is a passage about homosexuality, but only at first glance. After Paul speaks about homosexuality, he speaks about all of our sin. Yes, *our* sin. Did you notice the list in verses 29–31? "Wickedness," "evil," "envy," "deceit," "gossips," "slanderers." And then the adjectives: "insolent," "haughty," "boastful" and "rebellious toward parents," and the list goes on. So to the heterosexuals who think they're off the hook: Whatever your personal areas of struggle—your egos, your love of wealth and riches, your anger, your prejudices, your lust, your sexual struggles, your secret thought life, your self-centeredness—all have found a place in Paul's list of behavior that can dishonor God.

So many of these sins are not only more common but also more serious, more hurtful, and, I believe, worthy of greater condemnation than our topic today. This was precisely the apostle Paul's point in his passage from Romans 1 where he speaks about homosexuality. In Romans 2 he goes on to say, "Therefore you have no excuse, whoever you are, when you judge others; for in passing judgment on another you condemn yourself, because you, the judge, are doing the very same things" (v. 1). He begins by pointing to homosexual practice as one among many sins but ends by condemning those who pass judgment on others. Paul's ultimate goal is to help all of us

125

sinners see that we need a Savior—that Jesus came to save us from ourselves and from our sin, and that there is not one of us who stands righteous before God apart from Jesus.

Yes, I believe homosexual practice is not God's will for us. But homosexual people, I believe you have a special place in God's house, at God's table, in God's service. God knows your struggles and feels your pain. God has heard every prayer you have prayed. God knows that you feel, at times, like a square peg in a world built for round ones and that you want to follow, serve, and honor God, who knows the deepest longings of your hearts, your needs for acceptance, and for the love of your Heavenly Father. God does not condemn you today but invites you to radically commit your life to God, to be a whole person who finds the strength to live for God day by day. God will stand by you and help you as you seek to know and love God.

So, this is the invitation—as we conclude this chapter—to each of you, not simply to the homosexual, but to the heterosexual as well: Commit your life to Christ and long to be what he wants you to be and to do what he wants you to do. Invite the Holy Spirit to work in you, to make you into the man or woman God has called you to be, and seek to grow in the grace and knowledge of Jesus Christ, this day and forevermore. This is the essence of what it means to be a committed Christian, even in the face of the controversies of our day.

❈   ❈   ❈   ❈   ❈

Questions for Reflection

1. Paul repeatedly advises the churches to "agree with one another; live in peace" (2 Corinthians 13:11). How do we live by Paul's words when there are intractable disagreements that divide us? What should we pray for as our church struggles with divisive issues? How should we act toward people with whom we disagree?

2. What obligations do modern Christians have regarding the laws in the Old Testament? Read aloud this statement by biblical scholar Terence Fretheim and reflect on its meaning:

> God's gift of the law...remains integrated with the story of God's gracious activity in the ever-changing history of God's people. Law is always intersecting with life as it is, filled with contingency and change, with complexity and ambiguity. (*The Pentateuch*, Abingdon Press, 1996, p. 169)

An example of God's "gracious activity" is the deliverance of the Hebrews from Egypt (Exodus 12–14), which is followed by God's giving of the law on Sinai (Exodus 20). How are these two acts connected? Give some examples of biblical laws that reflect "life as it is" (in Leviticus 25, for example).

3. What did Jesus say about the laws in the Hebrew Scriptures? Read Matthew 5:17–20. What kind of obedience does Jesus expect? What does Jesus mean by righteousness? How is it possible to live in a way that exceeds the righteousness "of the scribes and Pharisees" who lived by the letter of the law (v. 20)? Read Matthew 5:43–48. How do you think the teachers of the law in his day reacted to Jesus' restating of the law found in Leviticus 19:18? Discuss what you think of Jesus' interpretation.

4. Read Luke 10:25–37, and in verse 33 substitute the word *homosexual* for the word *Samaritan*. Why was the Samaritan despised by the religious people of his day? What commandments does Jesus name as the greatest, the ones that encompass all others (see also Matthew 22:34–40)? How can we love our neighbor who is homosexual? Our neighbor who is homophobic?

5. Galatians 6:2 says "Bear one another's burdens, and in this way you will fulfill the law of Christ." Name some specific burdens borne by members of your congregation and include them in your prayers. Can you name burdens that you know others are bearing but which they may be unwilling or afraid to talk about? How can our community of faith make it easier to "bear one another's burdens"?

6. After a thorough check by social workers, a gay couple has been approved to care for foster children in their home. Both men are attentive and well-prepared for raising children. Their home provides an enriching atmosphere, and the children in their care thrive. Eventually they are allowed to adopt one of the "hard-to-place" children, a boy with severe learning disabilities and behavior problems. How can the church where they are members support this nontraditional family? Can this child and his adoptive parents expect the congregation to assist them and "[surround them with] steadfast love" as we promise to do at the baptism of children (*United Methodist Book of Worship* [Nashville: The United Methodist Publishing House], pp. 104–5)?

7. Write a prayer for the church in times of controversy and crisis.